Planning the Library Instruction Program

Patricia Senn Breivik

American Library Association

Chicago · 1982

Designed by Ellen Pettengell

Composed by Modern Typographers, Inc.,
in Linotron 202 Garamond

Printed on 55-pound Antique Glatfelter,
a pH-neutral stock, and bound in
10-point Carolina cover stock
by Edwards Brothers, Inc.

Library of Congress Cataloging in Publication Data

Breivik, Patricia Senn.
    Planning the library instruction program.

    Bibliography: p.
    1. Library orientation—United States.   I. Title.
Z711.2.B75 1982   025.5'6   82-8827
ISBN 0-8389-0358-4   AACR2

This book is dedicated to all the librarians
who participated in my seminars on educating
library users. They challenged me and were
the inspiration for this book.

. . . the activities of librarians become
meaningless unless they actually
effect changes in teaching and
learning.

B. Lamar Johnson
1948

Contents

v

Figures

Introduction

Library instruction is not a new phenomenon in librarianship. In 1876, Otis H. Robinson espoused the idea that the college librarian was more educator than custodian and argued that faculty and librarians should work together for the education of students.[1] The ability to use libraries and their resources as a means to personal and professional advancement has long been an underlying assumption in the concept of the public library as the "peoples' university." It was not until the 1960s, however, that library instruction became a widely held concern of public-service librarians. A number of ironies have been evident in this movement. First, library directors and library schools have had for the most part little or no interest in the subject, either in theory or in practice. Second, despite the increasing number of librarians active in library instruction and the increasing number of articles written on the subject, little or no progress has been made in the educational theory undergirding the movement or in the over-all improvement of programs. Despite these circumstances and despite the tightening of funds and reductions in staffing, the enthusiasm and number of those involved in such programs have never abated; indeed, they have continued to grow.

Progress has been hindered, however, by the lack of appropriate training for librarians. Although many school librarians have had some training in lesson preparation and writing learning objectives, by and large such training has been lacking. The greater problem, however, seems to be psychological: library collections and services have been traditionally developed in response to patron demands and needs. Library staffs normally react rather than initiate. While the profession has acknowledged the need to move ahead in areas of bibliographic control and automation, rather than wait for directives from its clientele, those librarians who have ventured into such areas as reader-advisor services, community-information centers, and instruction have been held suspect by colleagues who point out that libraries are not meant to function as social-service agencies or schools.

Well-established trends in education today argue against such a narrow view of librarianship. Concerns for lifelong learning, individualized learning, the nontraditional student, and decentralized learning all have implications for library services of the future. As far back as 1932, the Carnegie Corporation issued standards for college libraries that called for formal instruction in the use of the library and its bibliographic aids.[2] Forty years later the Carnegie Commission on Higher Education called for an expanded educational role for libraries and suggested a doubling of current funding levels to make it possible.[3]

In June 1978, after a conference on integrating academic libraries into the educational mainstream, a small group of major academic officers advocated an expanded educational role for libraries by issuing the following guidelines:

1. Universities and colleges should explore and feature the overall contribution of professional librarians to the general teaching function of their institutions through bibliographic instruction and other educational activities.

2. The concept of the library as a teaching library increases the effectiveness of the entire academic mission of academic institutions; it is a cost effective means of educating students; it is a flexible resource that can respond to the changing needs of students; it is an essential means for increasing the general research skills of students.

3. Further, it is important to emphasize that the teaching library and bibliographic instruction share a commonality of interest across colleges and universities of all sizes and missions.[4]

K. Patricia Cross, a nationally respected education researcher, spoke to the potential role of libraries in education at the 1979 American Library Association program meeting of the Library Instruction Round Table.

> Although I have been one of the staunchest advocates and promoters of individualized self-paced instruction in the schools, for the ultimate in self-paced instruction, nothing can compete with libraries. . . . Libraries are a unique national resource. They share some learning advantages with television, some with museums, some with schools; they supplement learning and provide in some instances the only opportunity of their kind in other cases.[5]

The question, then, is not whether or not educators will accept the library as a more dynamic partner in their endeavors, but whether or not libraries are ready to accept the challenge which already stands before them, and whether or not they have the vision, the ability, and the determination to move ahead. Such an effort will obviously necessitate a rethinking of library priorities; for particularly in times of tightening budgets, significantly strengthening one library program may well mean cutting back other activities. Perhaps such hard choices are at the heart of the problem: for whatever reasons (e.g., vested interests, fear, conservatism) most librarians have been willing to support library instruction only insofar as it does not inhibit other library activities.

There is an interesting anomaly here, for in its broadest sense much library instruction is imparted in the course of facilitating traditional reference work. Excluding the answering of directional and quick reference questions, the reference interview and subsequent development of search strategies with patrons is a personalized, one-to-one instructional dialogue, which many librarians would contend is library instruction at its best. But at its best in terms of what? Certainly not in terms of the numbers reached or the opportunity to have patrons systematically learn the scope and depth of information sources which can be of value to them in their studies and careers. Experience has shown that well-developed user-education programs increase the amount of work at the reference desk and the complexities of the questions directed there. Mundane, repetitious queries, on the other hand, inevitably become fewer. For as patrons master the elementary library skills and develop a greater awareness of the richness of the materials available, their expectations for library services and resources rise accordingly. On the other hand, because reference-desk interviews present opportunities to direct clientele to appropriate library-instruction activities, there is undoubtedly a complementary relationship between reference work and user-education programs.

This book is written, however, for librarians who are concerned with instruction in library use aimed at groups of people rather than one-to-one services. Even limited instructional programs have been well received simply because most individuals quickly perceive the practical advantages of learning to manage information effectively. But initial successes usually lead to greater demands. The minimal resources available for library instruction programs become quickly exhausted, while the pressures on the staff keep increasing. The question then becomes: how can the need for expanded library instruction services be met?

In response to this question, the Columbia University School of Library Service offered two advanced seminars during 1978 for academic librarians who were actively involved in instruction programs. These workshops, though thirty hours in duration, did not prove adequate to explore fully all the questions related to establishing and maintaining quality programs of library-user education. This book evolved from those workshops.

The book addresses school and academic more than public libraries because public library user-education programs have attracted less attention and public librarians have been far less involved in state and national library-instruction groups. This does not mean that there is no need for expanded programs in public libraries or that some good programs are not already in existence. For example, in 1976 public libraries in Texas were surveyed in preparation for a Texas Library Association meeting program; of the 47 that responded, 38 felt there was a need or demand for them to provide user education.[6] However, most of the basic concepts presented in the book are either directly applicable to all types of libraries, or could be adapted easily.

This book is the outgrowth of over ten years of involvement in library instruction. It is hoped that it will provide the reader with a clear understanding of the educational and political milieu in which library user-education programs must exist, as well as an understanding of the practical steps involved in planning and implementing them.

1. The Rationale for Library Instruction

The dilemma facing libraries in the decade ahead is whether they are useful enough to survive. Libraries have long championed the concept of free access to information; however, such access will be meaningless if the majority of citizens are ignorant not only of the quantity and scope of information available in libraries, but also of how to get that information and utilize it. No one would argue that it is sufficient merely to have medical facilities available; the knowledge of the availability of such services and how they can be secured is equally important. Yet librarians were surprised by the vehemence of the complaints made by lay people at the state pre-White House Conference meetings over the failure of libraries to inform the public of the availability of their resources and services. It is this failure, and the disuse of libraries that is its by-product, which have rendered their resources ineffective and threatens their survival.

School and academic libraries have a clearly specified role to play; they exist to support the missions of their parent institutions. Not only must these libraries define their role in support of the learning, teaching, and research functions of their institutions, but they also must make their faculties and administrators understand that role.

Educational institutions have long been dedicated to providing students with the means for advancing their careers, for improving the quality of their lives, and for preparing them for responsible participation in a democracy. To these needs, several others have been more recently added: to prepare people for lifelong learning, to answer the academic requirements of people with a wide variance in academic abilities and learning styles, to meet the needs of mature students, to help people cope with the information explosion taking place in their occupations and professions, and, last but not least, to help faculty cope with promotion and

1

tenure problems in crowded job markets—all this to be done with limited financial and human resources. These concerns are at the heart of the problems confronting education today. Libraries constitute far too large an investment not to be actively joining in the search for ways to deal effectively with these issues.

There is, however, no acknowledged statement of educational philosophy upon which library efforts can be shaped for attack. In recognition of this need, in June of 1979 the ALA Library Instruction Round Table membership, representing all types of libraries, endorsed two major projects. The first of these actions established a Task Force on Instructional Theory which is to formulate a theoretical basis, including definitions of concepts and taxonomies, relating library-user education to societal needs and educational activities. The second project charged the Task Force with developing goals and objectives for programs of user education in support of formal and informal education. These projects should provide direction to independent library-instruction programs and should help educational leadership—including library directors—to understand how libraries can support the educational goals of their institutions more directly and aggressively than they have in the past.

Library Instruction and Educational Quality

Library instruction can support teaching by addressing itself to the generally accepted characteristics of quality learning/teaching experiences which were spelled out at some length in a paper presented at the Spring 1978 meeting of the Midwest Academic Library Consortium at Ball State University in Muncie, Indiana.[1]

First, *a good learning experience imitates reality*. Once students graduate, no one is going to lecture them every time they need to learn something new on their jobs. No one is going to hand them a reading list. No one is going to put books on reserve for them in the public library. Traditional teaching methods no longer apply.

When students gain an awareness of the literature in their fields, learn the access to it, evaluate it, and utilize it, they are prepared for the postgraduation, real-life situations they will encounter. Library instruction must prepare them to cope with the multimedia information resources that are so much a part of society today. It must prepare them to utilize the mass media that will bombard them everywhere they go. Faculty and librarians working together can help students learn how to deal with the realities of the world's vast, multitudinous store of information. A positive learning experience must be grounded in reality.

Second, *a good learning experience is active not passive.* The lecture method, even if it allows time for questions and answers, does not meet this criterion. It is the essence of passivity. Educators have said for years that students should be provided with opportunities to learn by discovery—by developing concepts from specific incidences and in varying contexts, by starting with an initial problem and thinking it through themselves. Library or research skills obviously have a part to play in this process. Once students have acquired basic information-handling skills, they can begin to frame questions, to find the information that relates to these questions, and then to decide what is important or what needs to be done with the information they have uncovered.

Third, *a good learning experience is individualized.* Young people reach college campuses with a wide range of academic abilities. Open-admission policies, which guarantee entrance to college to virtually any high-school graduate, as well as the large numbers of students who have learned English as a second language, have exacerbated the problem. While some differential placement is generally the rule in freshman English courses, in other subject areas classes may well contain both academically well-prepared students and those who are almost illiterate in English.

No one instructional approach can be effective with such a wide range of needs. No one reading list can be effective with thirty students of widely ranging abilities. Circumstances force serious educators to consider ways to individualize the learning process. One approach is to take students directly to libraries and to other resources in the wider community. In that way students can deal directly with topics close to their special areas of interest, and materials can be varied to accommodate individual reading levels. By concentrating on magazine articles rather than books, for example, a student with a reading deficiency can find time to go over the material repeatedly until it is mastered.

Fourth, *a good learning experience makes provision for a variety of learning styles.* Some students learn best by listening, some by seeing, some in a lab situation; some work better in groups and some individually. Once faculty free themselves from the lecture, the textbook, and the reading list, and start looking for alternate approaches that utilize multimedia resources, multiple approaches to learning can become a reality.

Fifth, *a good learning experience is up to date.* The rapid obsolescence of most information is well documented; educators, in fact, have been saying for some time that the only valid object of education today is to concentrate on the processes of learning rather than on content.

The current catch phrase is *lifelong learning*. Almost every school and college pay at least lip service to this goal. Public libraries have long been responding to informal learning needs by providing adult independent-learning programs, reader advisors, and just plain, in-depth reference service.

Library instruction is essential to lifelong learning. Education for life-long learning begins to become a reality when people acquire an awareness of the literature in their chosen fields and learn how it is available, how they can gain access to pertinent information from that literature, how to evaluate it, and how to organize and use it. Such learning goes a long way toward ensuring that education will not stop once students receive their diplomas. Moreover, most studies show that 50–80 percent of what is learned in courses is forgotten by students within a year,[2] adding impetus to the need to prepare people for lifelong learning.

The concern for lifelong learning has reached international proportions. On November 26, 1976, the UNESCO Recommendation on the Develop-ment of Adult Education was adopted by the General Conference of the United Nations Educational, Scientific and Cultural Organization (UNESCO). This document pulls together and interrelates most issues relating to the development of a meaningful and effective network of adult education and lifelong learning in nations throughout the world.[3] In the same year Senator Walter F. Mondale of Minnesota introduced lifelong learning provisions to the Senate for inclusion in its education legislation.[4] Although the results of these actions will not be evident for years to come, it is clear that there will be a continuing shift from the ideal of universal terminal education to that of universal lifelong learning. Lifelong learning can begin during formal schooling years—particularly through the de-velopment of information-handling skills. The heaviest burden will ulti-mately fall on public libraries.

Sixth, psychologists tell us that *students learn best when the environment is least threatening*. Once teachers adopt learning/teaching approaches in which students learn by discovery, by working a problem out, students are relieved of the pressure of trying to figure out what their teachers "really" want. Students taught by traditional approaches spend a good deal of time trying to figure out just what it is that their teachers want them to accomplish—just as librarians at the reference desk do when students come in with assignment questions that neither the librarians nor the students can understand.

Allowing students to learn by directly exploring materials provides a positive learning experience, which, educators tell us, is one of the best ways to increase motivation to learn. Students can also better see the relationship between the process they are pursuing (particularly if it is pointed out to them) and what will face them once they leave school. Such an approach requires teamwork between librarian and teacher. By directing students, getting them started on a project, and then exposing them to the literature to find out on their own, instructors become facilitators of learning. (Something librarians have known about for quite some time.)

These six elements of high-quality learning provide a rationale for library instruction. They bring about the possibility for personal inquiry into particular subjects. Only when classroom instructors and librarians cooperate in this endeavor can the educational process take place at its best.

Cost-Effectiveness of the Instructionally Active Library

Defining purpose will help make school and academic libraries more attractive resources to those controlling the purse strings. Too many administrators think that libraries are a bottomless pit, exhausting all available financial resources. However, once libraries are perceived as dynamic tools that can be effectively employed to achieve the educational goals of their institutions, the attitudes of administrators may change significantly. The president of Earlham College has argued that libraries can offer academic administrators a cost-effective means to support quality education and provide an important area of flexibility for the tight budget years that lie ahead.[5] While a position added to one school or department of the institution will only increase program quality within that one unit, he commented, the addition of one librarian at an instructionally active library like Earlham's can support faculty in many areas, increasing the overall efficiency of faculty efforts and program quality. This cost-effective placement of a position also allows for flexibility in meeting changing student needs in the future. If a position is placed in a school or department which later suffers a significant drop in enrollment, it is difficult to shift and retrain the faculty member to contribute effectively in another academic area. It is much easier for librarians to adjust their instructional efforts to accommodate fluctuating student demands.

The priority of schools and colleges is for quality teaching/learning. University libraries have long been acknowledged as necessary for research. The role of library instruction as related to research has not been so clearly acknowledged, though instances proving this relationship are relatively easily available. Several years ago, for example, Daniel Johnson, then director of the Sangamon State University Middle-Sized Cities Center in

Springfield, Illinois, discussed ways in which librarians contributed to the successful completion of center projects. For one of the early projects, librarians provided in-depth instruction on relevant information sources. Johnson concluded:

> The bottom line of that incident was that it constituted a major savings in the time required to do the literature review. We figure that we saved upwards of three weeks for five or six persons involved in that project, simply by asking the two librarians to take us on a short-cut to the materials. They did it in a way that we could never have done it on our own, and so we have used that as a model for other projects that the center undertakes.[6]

This example shows library instruction at two different levels. The librarians created a learning situation in which the faculty members, the researchers, and the students were made aware in an efficient manner of the range of information sources relevant to the project. At the same time learning was going on in the affective domain: i.e., the researchers were seeing librarians as valuable members of their team who showed them how to gain more complete access to pertinent information while saving precious hours of research work. In other words, librarians could help them do what they wanted to do better and more quickly; librarians made the project more cost efficient.

It should need no underscoring that as money for education continues tight, the more ways in which a particular library supports the educational goals of its institution and the more people who perceive it as doing so, the better will be its position with other units. The libraries that are integrated into the educational mainstream and are thereby actively involved in supporting the educational goals of their institutions will fare better than their more traditional counterparts. The task for public libraries will be even more difficult if they are to meet the ongoing educational needs of an extremely heterogeneous clientele and make their constituency aware of the unique role they are prepared to play.

2. The Politics of Library Instruction

Despite the educational justification for library instruction, few campuses or schools welcome it unreservedly. Though community-rousing athletic programs, off-campus offerings, and programs in the health professions which are often helpful in offsetting declining enrollments may marshal support, in times of serious budgetary constraints the climate is not conducive to the introduction of new projects. Libraries, expensive operations in any case, are suspected of merely seeking more funds if new or expanded user-education programs are suggested. In truth, such programs *have* at times been promoted in order to justify budget increases.

Winning Library Staff Support

The first order of business in establishing a library instruction program is to gauge the level of support within the library itself. How prepared is the staff to assume new educational responsibilities, and what resources can the library redirect into such undertakings? Unless support within the library is strong enough to make the staff itself reorder priorities, it is most unlikely that support can be won from the institution of which it is a part.

Library instruction can enhance the prestige of the library in the school and on campus, can make it a more dynamic and visible component of the institution, and can underscore the fact that librarians are genuinely contributing members of the faculty. Why, then, does it receive so little enthusiasm, if not hostile response, from so many librarians? One must remember that not everyone likes change and that often people are fearful of

7

it. User education is a far cry from the quiet, ivory-tower type of environment that at one time attracted many people into the profession. In some cases staff members may have legitimate fears that they will be "forced" to stand up in front of large groups and teach if a major program gets under way. Certainly they have every right to expect that other activities will have to be adjusted, and perhaps favorite projects neglected, in favor of this new "fad." Even for librarians who are supportive of the concept, there are ego risks involved (e.g., what if the students do not like them?).

An element of jealousy may also exist. Librarians actively involved in instruction may be perceived as being "out there" having all the fun with classroom faculty, wasting lots of time at meetings, and probably gaining a real advantage in terms of promotion and tenure, while other colleagues have to stay behind doing the necessary behind-the-scenes work without which the library cannot function. Who will get all the praise and letters from grateful faculty? Certainly not the cataloger. Support staff—those who are in fact "holding down the fort"—are also apt to feel unappreciated in their roles.

Library staff may also fear having a new competitor for resources within the library. Although funds for library instruction may be garnered from savings created by more efficient operation, more frequently difficult internal budget reallocations will be necessary. Even those reallocations will eventually prove insufficient.

It is impossible to eliminate all of these concerns; some library personnel—for whatever reason—will never be active supporters of user-education programs. The goal should be to keep them from being active detractors, so that they will, for the most part, not be detrimental to the program during times of planning and priority-setting. Enthusiasts should remember that not everyone can be changed into a supporter. They should take time to listen to the concerns of the nonsupporter, and to understand the legitimate operational and emotional doubts being expressed. Enthusiasts should also make it clear that not everyone need participate in the program.

If the support of particular persons is crucial, one approach is to get behind a project in which *they* are especially interested. The goodwill that is generated may have some reciprocal effect. An above-board manner is appropriate, since it is unlikely that ulterior, albeit noble, motives will not be perceived.

When support does come from other quarters, be sure to share the glory; indeed, when possible give credit to others. For example, if the head of reader services, who is not an active supporter of the instruction program, allows time for planning or facilitates schedule changes to accommodate faculty requests for instruction, see that he or she gets credit for such helpfulness. When a faculty member offers to send a letter to the director in appreciation for the instruction, be sure to suggest that the letter mentions the head of reader services, without whose help it would not have been possible. Suggest, too, how nice it would be if the faculty member could speak or send a note of appreciation directly to the head of reader services.

Last, but perhaps first in importance, is the ongoing need to have all librarians and support staff understand how their work contributes—indeed, is necessary—to the instruction program. Efforts to this end can be built into new staff orientations and staff-development programs; most frequently gratitude can be expressed by simply taking the time and trouble to commend an individual's work in person or in writing. A library-wide representative group of librarians and support-staff members should participate in setting objectives for the library instruction program, and the entire staff should be kept informed of its development. These last two efforts, more than anything else, will gradually build internal support.

Winning the Library Director's Support

The director of the library is, of course, a key figure. The director's involvement may run the gamut from providing for a director of instruction activities, to ensuring rewards for those involved in the program, to being personally involved in planning or implementation. Certainly the active support of the director is necessary in negotiating support for user education outside the library.

Despite the serious interest in library instruction in the profession, library directors who are aggressive supporters of the educational role of librarians can be numbered on two hands. The reasons are not hard to understand. Few have had training in education. There are few models among other directors. There is little documentation on the actual value of such programs to students or to the total library program. A multitude of problems presses the director each day. Since many of them are caused by an eroding financial base, a new labor-intensive service, which is hardly being clamored for by faculty, is far from attractive.

In the case of a director who is neither strongly for nor strongly against library instruction, the best approach is to develop a positive, realistic plan that does not eliminate regular services or require more than the most modest of funds, if any. A careful culling of library and education literature will produce some good articles by academic officers and library directors supporting an expanded educational role for libraries, and it may be appropriate to bring a few of these to the attention of the director once his or her interest is piqued. Monitor the results carefully for submission in report form to the director, and make sure that any positive feedback from students, faculty, and/or department heads reaches the director. In the long run, indications of improved student performance after library instruction or growing interest on the part of classroom teachers will probably go the farthest toward gaining the active support of the library director.

Winning Faculty Support

In many ways the faculty are at the root of the success or failure of the user-education program. Efforts directed at faculty have payoffs that are potentially far greater than those aimed at students. Faculty are usually around longer than students, and so there is a better chance to build effective relationships. Once they are supporters of library instruction, they can reach many students each year by giving assignments that encourage library use, thus setting the stage for effective library instruction. The example that faculty set as active library users themselves will be influential. Because of their involvement in setting department and graduation requirements, faculty members are in a position to win a permanent place for library instruction in the curriculum. Finally, they may well be not only capable but also willing to do some library instruction themselves (perhaps with a little initial help from a librarian), thus expanding the instructional potential of the program.

Librarians can be resistant to change, and faculty can be inflexible as well. Even where instructors are theoretically convinced of the value of library use to their students, there may still be some stumbling blocks to their commitment to library instruction. It requires a fairly healthy ego to encourage one's students to seek out all the existing information in one's field: what if the students read something that contradicts what the professor teaches—especially if the writer is better known and more respected? Librarians need to be sensitive to such nuances and exercise the same tact as they do at the reference desk when readers are embarrassed about how much help they need. Larry Hardesty's article on the resistance of teachers to innovation, especially library instruction, is well worth reading.[1]

It is best to play to strength. The goal of reaching all faculty and students should not blind librarians to the reality that some faculty will never be "won over." Better than a shotgun approach aimed at all faculty is a focus on groups who appear to be sympathetic to library instruction. To work extensively with a few faculty and develop a comprehensive or model instruction program may pay off in the long run.

One approach is to compare performances of students who receive library instruction and those who do not and thus bring recognition to the faculty member and librarian who implemented the program. This approach may also be the most effective way of getting a component of the user-education program formally adopted into the curriculum. Success in one particular curriculum area may then be adapted for use in other academic programs as well.

Influential faculty members may warrant special attention. Faculty nearing the time for decisions on promotion or tenure are also good targets, as are those who are having to retrain because of changing enrollment patterns or changing directions in academic emphases. New faculty should receive special and immediate attention. In all of these cases, the instructors may prove particularly receptive to any idea that holds promise for enhancing their performances as teachers.

Similar opportunities may be created when a major upheaval or change occurs that affects the entire institution. The initiation of an open-admissions policy or competency-based education, a sudden influx of foreign students, etc., cause faculty to rethink their courses and teaching strategies. An enterprising librarian may be able to get a foot into the educational doorway at such moments.

Librarian-Faculty Liaison

Assigning librarians the responsibility of establishing ongoing relationships with faculty members within specific subject areas has proved especially effective. (Besides subject-based liaison, similar arrangements with selected units on campus such as instructional development, study-skills centers, and computer centers may prove worthwhile.) These liaisons are usually based upon subject expertise of the librarian at the level of the BA or MA; however, some librarians will have to assume liaisons in subject areas in which they have not had formal training—this often happens in the sciences. Nurturing such relationship requires initiative and hard work on the part of librarians if the liaison role is to develop meaningfully. Indeed, the whole question of suitable degrees needs to be rethought once librarians seek to become more involved in teaching. The ACRL standard, which considers the MLS as the terminal degree for academic librarians, loses credibility when librarians are teaching side-by-side with faculty members who generally possess a doctorate and are expected to do research and publish. This lack of comparable credentials places librarians on a lower level of prestige within the academic setting. The situation is different with school and public librarians who usually are as well or better educated than those they are serving.

Obviously, informal faculty contacts will always be important to library operation, but librarians who think such contacts can substitute for the development of delivery and communications planning are naïve. In the first place, some librarians are more comfortable with such informality than others. Such an approach is also extremely time-consuming. If more structured approaches are excluded, informal contact can convey the idea that the librarian has nothing better to do than to sit around and chat all day. All available avenues for contact should be considered, and the type of communication should be a carefully matched to the particular situation.

If, within the library, the liaison role is not carefully thought out and articulated, uneven service, totally neglected service levels, and much wasting of valuable time in informal explorations with a limited number of faculty may result. Librarians should have a clear idea of the kind and level of services they are prepared to offer. The liaison role may well vary from institution to institution, but in each case thought should be given to the appropriate involvement of the liaison librarian in the following areas:

1. Collection development
2. Curriculum planning
3. Faculty development
4. Faculty research
5. Library instruction
6. Library promotion.

Given the normally high ratio of faculty to librarians, planning is essential if service is to be delivered efficiently.

Suitable occasions for the liaison librarian to work with faculty must be found. Liaison opportunities such as the following should be considered:

1. Participation of librarians in departmental faculty meetings
2. Participation of faculty (or faculty and students) on a library committee
3. Participation of library director on an academic council
4. Participation of librarians in faculty governance
5. Participation of library support staff in staff governance
6. Preparation and distribution of a brochure on library services to faculty
7. Regular or occasional distribution of current library information in printed form to faculty

8. Placement of library information in school publications
9. Annual receptions for faculty; special receptions for new faculty

Certainly much detailed, factual information—as, for example, how to put materials on reserve and special library hours—is best put into written form so that personal contacts can be saved for more important, more professional concerns. There simply is not enough time for liaison work to be done on an informal, strictly one-to-one basis.

If strong supportive roles are to develop, faculty should have little concern about the seniority of the librarian who is liaison to their department. If the representative is changed too frequently or does not have sufficient time to meet their department's needs, they are bound to become uneasy.

Budgeting time is not a new problem to the school librarian who must always be accessible to all of the teachers in the school. But it is essential to set priorities: e.g., are there responsibilities that can be assigned to someone else, or can a specific task be dropped altogether in order to free the librarian for liaison-related activities? If all else fails, the librarian must be ready to explain honestly the reasons for the constraints on his or her time and to work with the teachers to determine how they can be served best with the time and resources that are available.

The more successful the liaison program is, the lengthier the planning process will be. At best, librarians will sit in on all curriculum-planning sessions and be able to promote the incorporation of suitable packages or requirements for library instruction while assuring that collection-development activities will reflect changing curriculum demands.

Winning Support of Administrators

Care should be taken to relate as effectively as possible with all power structures in the school or on the campus. Efforts at library instruction that support the nonacademic side of the institution may have short- and long-term benefits. For example, how can an academic library support the grantsmanship efforts of its institution? Frequently, development officers have well-established old-boy networks and extensive experience with a limited number of foundations and federal grant programs. Would some tactful instruction about resources available in the library (including appropriate state and federal documents) help to win funds for the campus, cut down on the duplication of expensive grantsmanship material, make contacts in the development office, or win friends elsewhere on campus? Such efforts may just be part of good library service, a prime example of how library instruction can help people do their jobs better as they learn about information available and how to access it. The library director will be in a position to point out such benefits to faculty and to major academic officers. Such efforts can show the library as an agent in bringing funds to the campus, not just in consuming them.

Academic and school administrators as well as their boards are seldom involved in the planning of user-education programs. This is unfortunate since such groups have major responsibility for the funding level of the library and are crucial to the development of an expanded educational role. If such groups are not well informed, they are also in a unique position to undercut programs of instruction.

The political situation at Sangamon State University is a case in point. Despite the national reputation of its teaching library, the board to which the university was responsible consistently put pressure on the administration either to pull money out of the library or to reapportion funds from personnel to materials. Lengthy discussions over a period of years showed a twofold problem. Despite the university's mandates for quality teaching and innovation, the board was uncomfortable with anything that did not fit the traditional role. It could see no reason for letting Sangamon's experiment continue since there was no hard data that validated the educational benefit of a teaching library. When both the president and the academic vice-president changed within months of each other, the board had its way. The story might have ended more happily if the library director had worked more effectively with the board staff from the very beginning, or if it had been possible for the director to cultivate the board members personally and apprise them of the library instruction program and its growing reputation (the board's executive director discouraged this). It is clear that by better documenting the results of its user-education program, the library could have done more to protect itself. Gut feelings that the program is proceeding well and notes of gratitude from faculty carry little weight when the financial chips are down. Part of the politics of being the new kid on the block in the teaching area is being able to prove that you have something to offer that is needed as well as wanted. Being too busy doing library instruction to evaluate it in terms meaningful to faculty, administrators, board members, and legislators is tantamount to committing suicide in these days of tightening funds for education. To understand the politics of library instruction is to communicate the benefits of the program to those who have the power to fund it.

In fact, whatever the developmental stage of the user-education program, it should be evaluated and documented and the results disseminated. Wherever possible, of course, it is advantageous to have faculty and others outside the library making the results of successful programs known. It is essential that the library staff, both professional and nonprofessional, give consistent signals concerning the program. Libraries are seldom known for their political clout; they need a well-unified front as they go out to compete for funds or to expand their educational role. Keeping the total staff informed of progress in the user-education program will help considerably in this process. Friends groups and any existing library advisory committees and boards should also be thought of as part of the home team and be kept well informed.

The other crucial aspect of building political strength for user education is totally within the control of library personnel: *the efforts of the program must be well targeted and limited enough to ensure unqualified success.* There is nothing more harmful to the development of a program than letting it expand so quickly that resources get too thinly spread. Far better to decline 50 requests for instruction so that 50 others can be done well than to carry out 100 instruction activities poorly. Such choosiness, of course, takes delicate handling. But if the planning process has been well documented, the limitations of the resources will speak for themselves, as will the library's plans to meet the needs of all students and faculty ultimately. The faculty members can then focus on the needs of the students in their particular departments and the ways in which the library user-education program can meet them. If instructors and librarians brainstorm, an interim solution may be found.

Winning Student Support

Almost nothing has been said in this chapter about students. In fact, students have little effect on the initiation of user-education programs. Their effect is largely a reactive one. Whether groups of students are particularly enthusiastic about a library-instruction experience or particularly negative, their feelings will be communicated to their instructors, and these attitudes in turn may seriously influence whether or not the instructors continue to encourage library instruction. In one instance, a professor who regularly surveyed students at the end of a management course received a unanimous response to the question, "What did you not expect to learn in this course which you found most helpful?" All students noted the unit taught by a librarian on foundation-funding sources. It became a permanent unit in that course. On the other hand, many slide/tape library orientation programs have sent both students and faculty away disgruntled.

Creative librarians may find ways to inject the library's presence into already existing or new student activities. For example, why not show the members of the Computer Club how the new technology functions in the library setting?

Winning Support in Planning Groups

Librarian involvement on key campus committees—particularly those involved in curriculum and academic standards—can prove extremely useful. Representation should be seriously sought on task forces and committees constituted to plan the future of the institution or improvement of instruction. On the academic cabinet, for example, the appropriate representative may be the library director; at the department heads' meetings it may be the school librarian. Such participation offers opportunities for articulating the educational role of the library. Such representation is particularly important when attempts are being made to formalize library instruction requirements on an institution-wide basis.

Winning Continuing Support

As must be evident by now, the entire professional staff could spend so much time politicking for user education that there would be no time left to provide the instruction. This problem can be alleviated if each gain is consolidated. Consolidating a gain may mean formalizing it in the requirements of a course or a department; it may mean having supportive institutional policies adopted, or at least having precedents set for following years. For example, if workshops for graduate assistants are tried one year and prove successful, the library director should attempt to get a policy adopted at the academic cabinet level to the effect that, henceforth, as part of the graduate assistantships, students must attend a library workshop unless they are excused by the librarian involved. Where secretarial workshops prove successful, arrangements should be made to present them annually, or from time to time as new groups of employees need orientation. Adding library instruction opportunities to relevant institutional activities should become a regular procedure.

If the campus has placement tests in English and mathematics for all incoming students, could a research/library test be added? At the University of Wisconsin at Parkside, where competency-based requirements must be met in four areas before the junior year, a requirement in library and research skills is included. The logical outcome of such a requirement would be a library-instruction course for those who cannot fulfill it. If the campus is committed to programs in lifelong learning, can a bibliographic instruction course be required as part of that goal? At one campus in Pennsylvania, for example, four such courses are regularly offered to meet the needs of students in the humanities, the social sciences, the sciences, and the professional programs. Self-paced library learning units can be effectively developed through use of a workbook or a computer program.

If a library unit cannot be included in graduation requirements, can departmental requirements be established? A library unit is required as part of the basic English course at many schools, and is part of the program in other disciplines as well. At one university in Illinois students are required to take both a pre- and post-library test as part of the core course in a management program. Even where a requirement at this level is impossible, a library unit may at least be established as a permanent part of an individual instructor's courses. Another approach might be through an agreement with a study-skills center, or a unit with designated responsibilities for educationally disadvantaged or foreign students, whereby workshops are regularly held or the students are regularly referred to the library for instruction.

Another way to formalize the opportunity for library instruction programs is to have a school or school system administer on a regular basis a standardized achievement test in library skills. Where such tests are automatically given as part of a series spread throughout the students' years of schooling, the administration and teachers will be concerned to see that the students get a good-enough exposure to library resources to perform adequately. The Higher Education General Information Survey (HEGIS) now queries institutions of higher learning about how many group presentations have been given in the library and how many people were present at the group presentations—an investigation that should serve as a spur to academic libraries.

Some librarians oppose the formalization of library-instruction learning requirements. Their concerns usually focus on such fears as: "People will then take it for granted," or, "Such requirements will lead to the same kinds of neglect that other educational requirements so frequently have." Of course such abuses are possible; however, they are not likely if the commitment to the library instruction program remains consistent within the library and the program is of a high quality. The whole point in formalizing library instruction requirements is to eliminate the need for repetitious politicking. The requirement guarantees the opportunity for the library to do its best.

Politics, of course, not only concerns what a library does, but what people know about what it is doing. Indeed, though the internal political concerns of the public librarians regarding user education have much in common with those of academic and school librarians, their external political concerns fall almost exclusively into the area of public relations.

In summary, then, when planning programs of user education and setting priorities within limited resources, careful thought must be given to political as well as educational ramifications, to making sure that what is done is done very well, and to documenting and disseminating the results of the program to build further support. Whenever possible, opportunities for library instruction should be formalized.

3. The Need for Planning: Setting Program Goals and Objectives

During the 1976/77 academic year, in preparation for a series of three statewide workshops on objective-setting, academic and research librarians throughout the state of Illinois were questioned about planning procedures.[1] Few had long-range plans and few regularly set objectives. School librarians in districts that required the setting of instructional objectives were an exception. The situation is similar in most other states.

Why Set Goals and Objectives?

The old story of the seahorse who did not know where he was going but rushed ahead until he ended in the shark's belly well illustrates the situation of many libraries and other educational organizations. Without the direction provided by clearly defined goals and objectives, it is difficult to allocate resources effectively, to make significant progress, to evaluate performance, to plan for the future, or to build outside support.

Setting goals and objectives is the first step—and an essential one—in seeking funds from state or local government bodies or from the parent institution. Such an enterprise is always basically a competitive one, since of course other agencies or units are also seeking funds for *their* programs. Regularly published self-evaluations are equally important.

As governmental units pass various versions of California's Proposition 13, and enrollments continue to decline, the ability of schools, colleges, and universities to articulate institutional goals in keeping with their charters or known educational needs will become increasingly important in competition for government funds.

Documentation of institutional achievements is the key. State and municipal governing bodies now face hard decisions about what programs to carry on and at what level of funding. To make such decisions, lawmakers will increasingly seek evidence of how well agencies are operating and to what extent they are achieving intended results. The need for institutions to document their contribution to broad-based public values was strongly underscored in an address in 1979 to the Illinois Association of College and Research Libraries by Illinois State Auditor General Robert Cronson:

> It may be argued that education should not be compelled to compete with horse-racing in the funding arena. However, that argument will not overcome the fact that resources are limited. All applicants for funding today are competitors. That competition must have a sound basis in performance, and that performance must be demonstrable. With specific reference to library services, the question can no longer be posed in terms of whether library service is desirable and contributory to public welfare. The question must be posed, in contemporary parlance, of whether library services are desirable "as compared to what."[2]

To ensure a favorable hearing on library needs, three elements are essential: (1) libraries must be able to demonstrate cost-effective operations; (2) their service objectives must be established in cooperation with representatives of the public the library serves, e.g., the faculty, the students, and the administration; and (3) services should have a demonstrable effect.

It must be remembered that the setting of broader objectives that relate to educational or community benefits runs contrary to long-established criteria for evaluating libraries, i.e., size of collection, number of staff, seating space, etc. Though these broader objectives are more difficult to document and measure, pressures to do so will continue to grow.[3] Arguments for additional funds to meet established collection or staffing standards will carry less weight in the future. Clearly articulating the library's unique role in supporting the stated goals of its parent institution (e.g., in preparing students for lifelong learning) may net additional dollars, particularly if the library can be shown to be able to contribute to the goals in a cost-effective manner. School library programs may have as stated objectives the improvement of reading levels or, for college-bound students, the satisfactory performance of research activities. Public library programs may adopt objectives which run the gamut from increasing adult literacy to improving community relations through providing meeting facilities or programming on cable television. The library's objectives should clearly support its constituency's stated or perceived goals. They should also produce results that can be documented.

A third level of competition occurs within the library itself. Priorities must be set among a multitude of necessary and desirable activities in both public and technical service areas. This inevitable competition makes the undertaking of major new services, such as library instruction programs, at any significant funding level almost impossible; for funding the new and unknown usually is done at the expense of established operations. Many instruction programs get started only if new monies are available, and too many die as soon as outside funding sources dry up. Only if an expanded educational role is a clearly stated goal of the library, and only if students, teachers, and administrators understand how this library goal supports other educational goals is it likely that the library will reallocate considerable funds to undergird user-education programs.

Issuing a document on library goals and objectives that includes a section on user education is a good first step, especially where teaching staff have demonstrated some beginning interest. It is best to present the section in the context of the effective utilization of library resources, for example, by providing assistance in locating and obtaining material. When library instruction is seen as one aspect of user-service activities, the user-education program can be developed within a known and existing framework.

Not surprisingly, however, the library record for setting objectives for education programs is as poor as for setting objectives in general. For example, in a 1976 survey of public libraries in Texas, 46 of the 47 libraries responding indicated that they had no written goals or objectives for their instructional activities, although only one indicated that it offered no type of library instruction.[4] Though most public libraries offer formal instruction, they seem not to perceive this function as separate from their other services. Notably, few public librarians are active in library instruction groups, and there are few publications about user education in public libraries. (And yet, philosophically at least, public libraries are far ahead of school and academic libraries in their attitude toward instruction.)

The necessary first step in planning for a quality instruction program, then, is the articulation of (1) the place of the program among library goals and objectives, and (2) the way in which the instruction program supports the over-all goals of the parent institution or the community.

Principles of Setting Library Instruction Goals

The goals of the library instruction program should always support the educational goals of the library's community or institution.

Educational service goals do vary from community to community, school to school, and campus to campus. Where the goals are not spelled out in official policy statements or mandates, a reading of existing documents will almost invariably give clear indications of program emphases and institutional priorities. Beginning-of-the-year addresses to teachers, letters to parents and alumni, college catalogs, and election platforms can all carry the message. Especially where institutional goals are not clearly articulated, statements of the goals and instructional objectives of the library need widespread endorsement. (If something is not acceptable to the library's clientele, far better to discover this fact before implementation of the instruction program.) In the case of public libraries, general community-needs assessments should be constructed so as to provide data for planning the instruction program. When user-education program goals and objectives are developed from the data obtained, the public library administrators should then take the user-education planning documents to the library board, Friends groups, and other representative groups for official endorsement.

The ACRL memorandum entitled "Guidelines for Bibliographic Instruction in Academic Libraries" (Appendix) is well worth reviewing. It does a particularly good job of spelling out how the program should be incorporated within the operations of the library.

The school or academic library need not spend too much, if any, time surveying the needs of its campus for library orientation and instruction. If librarians have been at all active in their institutions, they should already have gained a clear picture of needs from their contacts with instructors, their experiences at the reference desk, and the efforts at library instruction that have been already under way. The wisest course for them is to move ahead to preparing a profile of the groups to be served and their needs (see Chapter 4). The one valid exception to this rule may be the very large university setting; a 1976 article entitled "Community Analysis in an Academic Environment" by James F. Govan, presents a good overview of the problems and opportunity of the library's role within the wider academic community.[5]

Harvie Branscomb summed up the importance of setting goals. The solution to the problem of integrating library management and educational needs, he said, "consists in reworking the program of the library from the point of view that the primary concern of the library, as well as the rest of the college, is the effectiveness of the course of study."[6]

A Procedure for Setting Library Instruction Goals

In planning for the library instruction program, it is important to start with the goals of the parent institution (stated or unstated) and then develop instructional goals that support them. Goals in this context are defined as long-term desired outcomes, which, although they may never be reached, provide direction and focus for more finite objectives which have measurable outcomes to be accomplished within specified time periods—usually a year. One goal might be to make independent library users of all faculty and students and thus help to fulfill the college's goal of preparing its constituency for lifelong learning. Such a wedding of objectives provides a healthy framework with which to approach a particular academic department about creating a library unit in a core course.

Working within the framework provided by the goals for the instruction program, planning must next focus on determining the groups to be served and their information needs. The consequent preparation of learning matrices that can serve as the basis for setting instructional objectives is discussed in detail in Chapter 4.

A distinction should be made at this point between the two types of objective-setting which are referred to in this book. The library-wide goals and objectives and the goals and objectives for library user-education programs that are discussed in this chapter are operational or program-type objectives. The discussion beginning in Chapter 6 switches to consideration of instructional or learning objectives. Both types of objectives are concerned with clearly stating in advance how success or accomplishment will be measured. Both types of objectives have stated time frames after which evaluation is to be conducted. Both types sometimes state conditions or limitations under which the activity is to transpire. Both types are important to a successful program of library instruction.

Many program objectives will develop out of the learning matrices. However, the administrative reality of limited resources will necessitate postponing work on some objectives in favor of others. This setting of priorities is an extremely painful process. How can one ignore agreed-upon needs? Is it not better to do a little work in each area rather than concentrating on a few activities? Definitely not! There will always be more good things to be done than time or resources permit, and far too many librarians have learned firsthand the pitfalls of spreading their efforts so thin that they and those they are serving have been left frustrated and unsatisfied.

Setting priorities is a means of assuring that certain important outcomes will be reached, and that at the end of a period the library will have some accomplishment to point to with pride, a baseline from which to plan more far-reaching efforts. This difficult process of setting priorities among program objectives is covered in Chapter 5. The steps in the entire planning process are shown in Figure 1.

Focusing, then, on setting the goals and objectives for the library user-education program, the first question to be asked demands some imagination and optimism. Given the goals, mandates, major concerns, and emphases of the institution within which the library resides or the needs of the community it is to serve, what would a full-blown library instruction program ideally accomplish? The answers to this question should become the goals of the program. Possible goals might be:

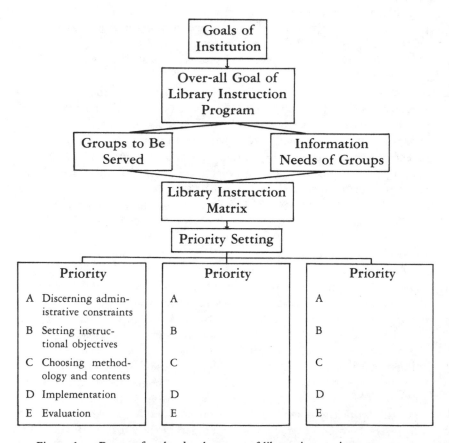

Figure 1.   Process for the development of library instruction programs

> To promote quality education on campus.
>
> To promote the use of library resources as a means of enhancing the learning/teaching process.
>
> To be actively involved in the learning/teaching process.
>
> To insure that campus research efforts are undergirded by efficient utilization of library resources.
>
> To serve as a center in the community for adult independent learning.

The value of setting these pie-in-the-sky goals lies not in the belief that they will ever be reached but in the direction and the opportunity for building staff support that they provide. It is unlikely that such long-term, lofty statements will ever elicit vehement disapproval from anyone within the library, the wider institution, or the community, particularly if the goals are publicized in terms that show how they relate to institutional goals or community needs. When broad goals are being set all library employees should be informed and their input solicited. This is the ideal opportunity for the user-education program to really become the program of *all* library employees, not just those who will be doing the teaching. Moreover, campus administrators and board members, having endorsed such program goals, will find it difficult to oppose concrete activities that support them.

Setting program objectives (as opposed to instructional objectives) should include as many people as possible. Management literature is clear on the point that participation in decision-making through setting objectives does much to build staff morale and to motivate staff toward improved work performance. Staff participation should not be lightly neglected. Even if a library director operates in a highly hierarchical manner, all possibility of goal- and objective-setting by the staff does not have to be precluded; boundaries can be set within which the process will occur, while the director retains ultimate veto power.

To streamline the procedure of setting objectives, a library may wish to develop worksheet formats. These will facilitate the identification of possible objectives, on all necessary matters, while providing for enough uniformity to allow for consolidation. An example of such formats appears in Figures 2 and 3. Such worksheets may be used for other areas of program or operational-objective writing, as well as for the user-education program.

The first worksheet (Figure 2) can be used to identify areas of concern among staff. In it, individuals identify a possible area for priority concern for the coming year, the reason why it is thought to be important, and the library goal that it supports. How the priority area might be turned into an objective to guide action can also be indicated.

RECOMMENDED PRIORITY WORKSHEET

Priority Area:

Rationale:

Library Goal That It Supports:

Outline of Proposed Objectives:

1. The *person* who is to perform the desired task or activity.

2. The *specific performance* to be employed in achieving the task or activity (i.e., what activities or tasks would be involved).

3. The *result* that will be measured to determine if the task or activity has been accomplished.

4. The *relevant conditions* under which the task or activity is to be performed (e.g., special funding, time elements, equipment, etc.).

5. The *criteria* (standards) to be used to measure the success of the result or performance.

Figure 2.   Recommended priority worksheet form

Worksheets permit two basic approaches. A planning committee can review them, combine similar concerns, omit some or add others, and then suggest a priority order for review by the entire staff. Or the planning committee can make the initial identification of priority areas, after which input can be solicited from the library staff.

Once there is general agreement on priority areas, each area should be assigned to an individual or a small task force for the development of objectives. The second worksheet (Figure 3) aims at flushing out the priorities into an objective format for developing an action plan. The

_____ objective for _____
(Year)

Rationale Library Goal/Objective	Activities for Accomplishment, Including Time Schedule	Person(s) Responsible	Measurement Accomplishment (How and By Whom)

RATIONALE:

LIBRARY GOAL:

OBJECTIVE:

EVALUATION:

_____   _____
Evaluator   Date

Figure 3.   Single objective worksheet form

worksheet demands that thought be given to the precise outcome desired and the ways in which, in detail, success will be measured. Then in a step-by-step fashion the necessary activities are outlined. Who is responsible for doing what, the time frame, and what, if any, special resources will be needed are indicated at each step. The worksheet allows room for a restatement of the rationale for the objective and the library goal it supports. It also provides space to indicate the result of the evaluation at the end of the designated time frame.

Once a set of objectives has been completed, the director, the head of library instruction, the library instruction committee, or another appropriate group should make the final decision about which objectives the library should adopt. Administrative or political constraints (see Chapter 5) that would make completion of an objective clearly impossible and the optimum number of objectives that are feasible are considered at this point. Figures 4 and 5 show a completed priority worksheet and a set of program objectives that might grow out of it.

It is useful to have the completed objectives easily accessible to staff so that everyone interested may know who is working on what at what point. Periodic progress reports and monitoring will assure that the activities are proceeding as planned; if not, staff members can be alerted to unforeseen difficulties in time to adjust the objective or its timetable. There is, in fact, nothing wrong with adjusting an objective if some unforeseen change occurs or if, through subsequently gained information, a miscalculation in the original assumptions becomes apparent; nor is there anything wrong in not achieving an objective provided that it is clear why the objective was not accomplished. The original time frame may not have been realistic, a serious budget cut may have precluded the procuring of necessary materials, a key person may have resigned, etc. If an objective is not successfully completed, the reason should be documented so that, in the next year, serious consideration can be given to whether the objective should be pursued, dropped, or modified.

Experience in program objective-setting decreases the likelihood of setting unrealistic objectives. Unless there is a major unforeseen problem, an objective agreed upon and fully planned will almost always be successfully completed. There are several sound reasons for this. First, everyone concerned has agreed on a clear path to follow. Second, when decisions must be made on a unit or individual basis, there is now a framework in which to make them. Most decisions in libraries involve choices among two or more good alternatives. Such decisions can now be made in keeping with agreed-upon objectives for the year. That is, rather than arbitrarily responding to requests or demands or performing on a first-come, first-served basis, the

RECOMMENDED PRIORITY WORKSHEET

Priority Area:
Production of library guides

Rationale:
Many need updating and others would be helpful for users.

Library Goal That It Supports:
To promote increased use of library resources as a means of enhancing the learning/teaching process.

Outline of Proposed Objectives:

1. The *person* who is to perform the desired task or activity.
   Liaison librarians

2. The *specific performance* to be employed in achieving the task or activity (i.e., what activities or tasks would be involved?).
   Evaluation of existing guides and revision or new production as needed.

3. The *result* that will be measured to determine if the task or activity has been accomplished.
   How many are produced and/or quality

4. The *relevant conditions* under which the task or activity is to be performed (e.g., special funding, time elements, equipment, etc.).
   Many are needed for beginning of semester.

5. The *criteria* (standards) to be used to measure the success of the result or performance.
   Evaluation by Publications Committee

Figure 4.   Completed priority worksheet

library can now decide to perform or not to perform an instruction activity on the basis of whether or not it will facilitate the accomplishment of the agreed-upon priorities for the year. Finally, the mere agreement that a certain objective should be pursued causes most people subconsciously to think and move in that direction.

Program or operational objectives usually are given a one-year time frame. Although there is no hard and fast rule about this, since appropriations are usually made on an annual basis, such a time frame is sensible. The setting of objectives should occur far enough in advance to allow for necessary staff changes and for earmarking sufficient dollars to meet the requirements of implementation. This means that objectives for the com-

1982–83 objective for PUBLIC SERVICES
(Year)

Rationale Library Goal/Objective	Activities for Accomplishment, Including Time Schedule	Person(s) Responsible	Measurement Accomplishment (How and By Whom)
RATIONALE: To inform patrons of library resources.	1) Appoint a coordinator to centralize production and/or revision of information sheets and pathfinders. July 1, 1982.	Jane Doe	1) Appointee on job.
	2) Review existing library information sheets and pathfinders to determine appropriate content, ease of use, format, etc. July 7, 1982–August 4, 1982.	Publications Committee and Jane Doe	2) Documented recommendations for changes.
	3) Determine number of new or revised materials needed in 2 above, and incorporate into activities for accomplishment. August 4, 1982.	Jane Doe in consultation with liaison librarians	3) Number to be produced listed under activities for accomplishment.
LIBRARY GOAL: To promote increased use of library resources as a means of enhancing the learning/teaching process.	4) Produce new or revised information sheets or pathfinders. August 4–29, 1982.	Liaison librarians	4) New or revised information sheets and pathfinders ready for distribution.
	5) Review information sheets and pathfinders for usefulness at the end of Fall and Spring semester. Review December 1982. Review May 1983.	Publications Committee and Jane Doe	5) Review completed.
	6) Write final report. June 1–July, 1983.	Jane Doe	6) Final report given to Director of Public Services
OBJECTIVE: To develop information sheets and pathfinders.	7) As needed, activities will be repeated cyclically beginning annually in August.	Jane Doe	7) Production of new materials for final report.

EVALUATION:

_____   _____
Evaluator   Date

Figure 5.   Worksheet showing program objectives

ing year will have to be set while those of the current year are being fulfilled. Obviously, objectives related to user education will have to be considered alongside other operational goals. A possible planning calendar for a school or academic library might be:

November: Receive suggested priorities worksheets from staff

December: Decide on most likely priorities and assign people to develop them on objective worksheets

Jan. retreat: 1. Review progress on current year's library-wide objectives
   a. Will the timetables on any objectives have to be revised?
   b. Will any objectives have to be carried over into the following year?
   c. Will any current planning objectives require implementation objectives for the following year?
2. Review drafted library-wide objectives for the coming year
   a. Are the objectives well thought out and feasible?
   b. Is there agreement on the appropriateness and importance of the objectives?
   c. Can all the objectives (plus carry-over ones from current year) be implemented in one year; if not, which should be postponed or eliminated?
3. Inform entire staff of tentatively chosen library-wide objectives for coming year

February: Develop divisional objectives

March: Develop departmental objectives

April: Develop personal objectives

May: Project necessary changes in staff assignments and budget allocations to implement objectives from the beginning of the next school year.

June 1–15: Evaluate current year's objectives

June retreat: 1. Review evaluation of current year's objectives; determine any need for continuance
2. Review tentatively adopted objectives for the coming year
3. Formally adopt as many objectives as are desirable and feasible

Summer: 1. Complete annual reports
2. Begin developing materials and conducting staff training necessary for implementation of objectives

July–Sept.: Begin implementation of objectives

A particular advantage of this calendar is that it allows the summer for preparing instructional objectives and materials and in some cases working with instructors. All will be in readiness before the beginning of the academic year, when there is usually a heavy demand for instructional support from the library but little time for planning on the part of either the librarians or the classroom teachers.

The final steps in the process of setting objectives are to evaluate the results as agreed upon in advance, to document the accomplishments, and to decide whether the objective needs further work or whether a new objective should grow from a prior one.

The importance of the documentation should not be underestimated. There is always so much to do that the stroking that is so necessary to the mental health of all members of the library staff—from the newest clerk to the director—is often overlooked. Evaluating the outcomes of objectives is a natural and appropriate way to point with pride at the library's accomplishments and to make sure that all involved feel appreciated—whether their role was direct or supportive. Moreover, documentation makes for interesting reading in annual reports and in reports to administrators. It provides a track record for the library: the library said it would do these things; the library has done them. It is a well-managed operational unit. Such a record will be useful when seeking support from outside sources.

4. Meeting the Needs of the Groups to Be Served

One of the first steps involved in planning programs of library instruction is to identify the groups to be served and to determine priorities among them. Although the process involved in this planning stage is similar for school, academic, and public libraries, the circumscribed nature of the school and academic community make this first stage a less complex one. References to the public library will, for the most part, be reserved until the end of this chapter.

User-education programs in educational institutions will obviously serve students and will usually serve the classroom instructors; but other groups and their needs should be considered as well: administrators, alumni, community groups, staff, parents. Thought should also be given to the needs of the library staff themselves.

The identification of groups to be served is further complicated by the need to differentiate among subgroups. For example, one cannot refer simply to students whether at the university or the elementary-school level. The differences between first graders and sixth graders makes it meaningless to place them under the same category. The same is true between the academically unprepared college freshman and the Ph.D. student in biology. On the other hand, since it is impossible to plan programs to deal with students on an individual basis, some generalizations must be made.

Fortunately, most institutions have a great deal of readily available information on their students. Enrollment figures by academic program, number of part-time versus full-time students, number of students at each grade level, number of students assigned to remedial classes or referred to skills centers, average age level, number of foreign students—all such statistics are helpful in defining the framework for the library user-education program. In small schools the librarian may well have enough

33

personal contact with students and teachers to have a firsthand knowledge of their varying needs. This may be as simple as knowing that all third-grade teachers present a unit on map reading, for which a library instruction unit might be appropriate. In larger schools, however, statistics may prove useful in establishing theoretical groups of students for planning purposes. Information should be available on the numbers of college-bound and vocational students, the number of students with below-average reading ability, and the most popular electives. High concentrations of students in one category should indicate targets for initial efforts, unless there is some political reason for taking some other approach.

Data on students must always be considered in conjunction with information on the goals, mandates, and priorities of the parent institution. Together, these sources of information should greatly assist in distinguishing and setting priorities. For example, if an inner-city college has a publicized commitment to its community, particular attention will need to be paid during the planning process to the ways in which library instruction efforts can reach out into that community. At other institutions this clientele might receive lowest priority. To take another example, an institution long known for academic quality but faced with declining enrollments might be newly concerned about student retention; in such a situation, the library user-education program should give particular thought to providing high-risk students with academic survival skills.

It is relatively easy to develop a comprehensive list of potential client groups for the instruction program. Differentiation within the groups becomes more difficult; there is no one right or wrong way of creating the subgroups. For example, one might separate undergraduate from graduate students and then divide the groups among the various subject disciplines. On the other hand, it might be just as reasonable to divide the student population by academic discipline and then separate each group into subgroups for undergraduates and graduates.

The structure of the individual institution will be a guiding factor. If, for example, librarians are assigned as liaison to academic programs, it makes more sense to divide first by discipline. Or, if the campus strongly differentiates between its undergraduate and graduate programs, has a graduate dean, etc., dividing first by level might be better. Breaking the institution down into smaller groups is simply a way of comparing and contrasting informational needs and setting instructional priorities. Any configuration that serves this purpose will do.

In the following paragraphs, the major constituencies for the library instruction program are discussed. The points raised are ones that should be considered within the planning process.

Groups to Be Served

Students

Though a library may wish to serve all students equally, the realities of limited human and financial resources dictate that the goal of reaching them all will have to be accomplished in steps, i.e., by meeting intermediate objectives. Therefore, a listing of subgroups of students is essential. Figures 6 and 7 show two possible breakdowns for academic library planning. Knowing the numbers involved at least vaguely can also prove useful, since the purpose is not only to ensure that no group is inadvertently omitted from the program but also to set priorities for program development.

Graduate assistants and teaching assistants (school librarians might wish to have a separate group of student teachers or teacher aides) deserve special attention. Not only do these students have special information-related needs, but also they frequently are in a unique position to support library instruction programs. Since they are just beginning to have academic responsibilities that transcend their own studies, they are likely to be open to any activity which can enhance their success. Moreover, they are in a strategic position to reinforce library approaches to faculty and, in some cases, students.

Academically less prepared students form another subgroup that warrants special consideration. Whether the problem is caused by poor preparatory education, access to English only as a second language, or lack of motivation, such students have particular problems that will challenge an effective user-education program. The sizes of these groups and the stance taken toward them by the parent institution should affect their place in the list of priorities. If a skills or study center exists, some thought should be given to using it as a vehicle for library instruction and/or for referring students to the library in small groups for instruction.

The particular needs and rights of handicapped students have received a great deal of attention in recent years. If the parent institution has a large number of handicapped students, such students may well be listed as a subgroup. Otherwise, it may prove wiser to provide instruction on demand to individuals or very small groups who are handicapped.

Student workers in the library may also be considered to be a special subgroup (of students or of library employees). Obviously, they will have learning needs relative to their jobs as well as to their academic program. Student workers have special opportunities for mastering library skills. A better overall understanding of the library and library resources may also increase their motivation and levels of satisfaction in their library work.

Graduate Assistants

Teaching Assistants

Graduate Students

    Professional schools
      1.
      2.

    Liberal arts schools
      1.
      2.

Student Workers in Library

Academically Disadvantaged

Undergraduates

    By various schools and departments
      1.
      2.

Figure 6.   Student breakdown I: By level

They may become promoters and advocates of library instruction in their classrooms.

On academic campuses the needs of the more mature student, who may have full-time employment or family responsibilities, will vary considerably from the needs of traditional, dorm-residing eighteen-year-olds. Frequently, they are identified by their enrollment in weekend and night classes. Where this kind of natural division occurs, it would be inexcusable to present the same library instruction workshop as a shotgun approach to the needs of "the average" student. Many campuses also sponsor off-campus courses. Supposedly, such courses have the same quality as those offered on campus. What, if any, library services are available to students enrolled in such courses, and what are their library instruction needs?

Faculty

Library instruction for faculty covers three areas: (1) logistical information, such as how to put materials on reserve and how to check out AV equipment; (2) the information and skills needed to pursue research

ENGLISH STUDENTS

General composition courses (open to all)

academically prepared

academically disadvantaged

General literature courses (open to all)

academically prepared

academically disadvantaged

Courses for majors

composition

literature

criticism

research

independent studies

BUSINESS STUDENTS

Figure 7.   Student breakdown II: By academic discipline

in teaching and publishing; and (3) the ways in which library instruction can support instructional objectives. It is well to remember, of course, that among faculty familiarity with the library can range from those who have never set foot inside to those who are active users and supporters.

Some subgroups of faculty deserve particular consideration. New faculty, for example, have immediate and pressing problems that present a unique opportunity for developing friends for the library and the library instruction program. Part-time faculty, who work full-time elsewhere and usually are only on campus once a week, present particular problems and challenges. Faculty assigned to work with special groups of students, either within the mainstream of the curriculum or in skill development or in research centers, will also need to relate to the instruction programs of the library in a different fashion from that of regular classroom teachers. Each of these groups and their needs should at least be considered in the planning stages of the instruction program, whether or not they eventually receive priority ratings.

Librarians need to recognize that library instruction is intrinsically threatening to many faculty. First, it encroaches upon the very limited time they have with their students. Second, the students may acquire knowledge about library resources that is beyond that of the professor. Third—and by far the most serious threat—students may well find and study materials which go beyond or contradict what the professor believes and teaches. This threat is particularly intimidating to professors who are insecure because they are new in teaching or have been giving the same basic lecture for years. It is far more comfortable to have students exposed only to the information that the professor assigns or imparts in lectures. Although it is extremely doubtful that such concerns will ever be articulated as reasons for not supporting library user-education programs, astute librarians will keep them in mind. Librarians may find appropriate ways of reinforcing faculty self-confidence. Library instruction that is offered as a means of enhancing faculty's own teaching and academic successes is bound to win converts.

Initially, most library instruction programs revolve around individual faculty members who are cooperative. As a more comprehensive program is planned, it will usually focus on particular departments or units where the majority of the faculty have shown openness to initiatives made by the librarians.

It is worth pointing out that even faculty who regularly use the library and campaign for increases in the acquisitions budget will not necessarily support library instruction. Many will be "sure" that their students already know how to use the library, and will not be sympathetic to library instruction unless, of course, the fact that their students do need library instruction is somehow documented.

Administrators and Board Members

Most administrators need to gain an appreciation of how library instruction can support the educational goals of their institutions. Given the time constraint under which administrators work, for them most library instruction will have to be done on a one-by-one basis. Members of governing boards, and, when appropriate, city council members and legislators should also be sought out. Educating these groups to the educational potential of the library should be considered an important priority in planning the library instruction program.

There is no more natural audience for the appreciation of the educational value and desirability of library instruction than school and college administrators, board members, and elected officials who are concerned with the broader goals of public and higher education. The conflict between this broader perspective and that of the instructors who tend to focus on the mastery of a particular subject was well summarized at a conference on the undergraduate and lifelong reading interest held in 1959:

> The stated aims of the institutions of higher learning are almost always those which would best be served by the intelligent use of books and reading. The training of the whole mind; the development of the student's powers of original thinking and analysis; the exercise of the student's imagination; the promotion of sensitivity, aesthetic appreciation and understanding; the recognition of recurring problems of life adjustment; the deepened understanding of one's self and of others; and so on—surely these are aims which transcend the narrow limits of any one discipline and call for training in the use of tools and concepts, techniques and viewpoints which will foster continuing self-education. But the disturbing fact to which the conferees constantly returned is that of the very real conflict which exists between these admirable long-term goals, and the immediate goals of the individual courses.
>
> The reality with which students, faculty members and librarians are all too familiar is that the individual course concentrates upon a narrowly defined body of knowledge or system of analysis with little relevance to other courses and disciplines, and makes but limited and unimaginative use of books. Course content and reading assignments are almost never designed to promote the kinds of book use that would be of value beyond the final examination.[1]

Not only is there a good potential match of educational concerns between library and administrative/governing groups, but the latter groups, as discussed in Chapter 2, are in unique positions to further or hinder the development of the entire library program.

Staff

On every campus and in every school there are support staff: secretaries, administrative aides, and research assistants. All of them have institutional responsibilities that frequently relate to library resources and services. In many cases their job performances can be improved if they know how to take advantage of library or other information resources to which the librarians can direct them. Their needs should be considered in any planning of a total library user-education program. Secretaries, in particular, deserve attention. Because they frequently exert a good deal of influence on their bosses, their perception of the library may well have a ripple effect.

Community

A tax-supported institution has a built-in responsibility to the community that surrounds it, whether the community aids the institution directly or is only part of a larger body that provides support. Even private institutions nowadays find it difficult, if not dangerous, to ignore those who live around them. The extent to which the library's community outreach efforts are considered a priority should be clear from the tone set by the administration. Yet capitalizing on community relationships will require some thought in the planning of the library instruction program. Local high school students are a natural target for most college, university, and public libraries. Local businesses are also important. Thought should also be given to social and church groups as well as to the local media. Certainly school libraries will have to give serious consideration to parent and teacher organizations in planning their instruction programs.

Alumni

Whether a Friends of the Library group exists or not, some thought should be given by academic libraries to instruction activities for alumni. During planning, the library should consciously consider whether particular activities should be planned for alumni, whether they should be planned in conjunction with other alumni activities, whether alumni are an important constituency in community-based instructional activities, or whether they should be ignored.

Library Personnel

The value of professional and support-staff development in libraries is drawing increasing attention. The ideal situation from a management perspective is to have all employees working to full capacity. Library instruction programs are bound to create staff pressures. An increasing portion of the librarians' time must be spent working directly with faculty and students and in preparing for group presentations. This added responsibility will in turn require that others take on many of the clerical and supervisory tasks previously performed by librarians. Furthermore, when we consider the rapidly changing technological and political milieu in which libraries must operate, it is clear that consideration of the role of the library staff must receive high priority when establishing the library instruction program.

Developing a Matrix

It is possible, after determining subgroups to be served, to develop a learning matrix for library-user education. Subgroups are listed down the left margin, their information-handling learning needs across the top.

What kinds of needs are listed? All kinds! The needs cluster at three different levels of expertise—the orientation level, the basic skills level, and the advanced or subject-specialization level. At each level there are six basic types of learning needs:

> Attitudinal learning
> Logistics
> Resource logistics
> Organization of information
> Resources available
> Search strategies.

Attention will be given to each type of learning need in Chapter 9, which deals with contents selection and timing.

General Matrices

For practical reasons, it is desirable to prepare two sets of matrices, one at a general level, the other concerned with definite skills and resources. At the initial stages of planning, it may be advisable to deal with fairly large groups and more general statements of needs (Figure 8). The general matrices have several uses. When comparisons are made among the learning needs of the various subgroups, patterns emerge. Some needs appear only in a few instances; others appear for all the subgroups.

The patterns that emerge in the general matrix lay the groundwork for developing the instruction program. One criterion for priority rating among instruction needs might be those held in common by a majority of the groups. The matrix will affect scheduling, for the needs held by many groups should be addressed early in the educational process (with alternative learning opportunities provided to ensure adequate coverage), while other, less universal learning needs should be addressed later, when the program can build on a common foundation. Matrices can also help to ensure that work will not be needlessly replicated. Needs held in common by two or more groups can be worked on by one librarian or group of librarians, and only minor adaptations will be required from group to group. In summary, these matrices can:

LEARNING NEEDS												
GROUPS TO BE SERVED	Orientation	Basic Skills	Basic Reference	Subject Research	Advanced Bibliography	Special Collections	Search Strategy	Survival Skills	Term-Paper Skills	On-Line Searching	Etc.	
Undergraduate Students												
Graduate Students												
Faculty												
Administrators												
Campus Staff												
Library Staff												
Community												
Alumni												

Figure 8.   General matrix

Help to designate high-need areas
Help to sequence learning experiences logically
Help to avoid unnecessary duplication of effort
Help to avoid replication of learning experiences by students.

More than one learning approach is necessary to meet broad-based needs.

Specialized Matrices

After areas with the greatest need are designated, those identified for priority attention in the coming year can be further expanded. Specialized matrices proceed from the broad needs of the subgroups to individual learning experiences that are appropriate (Figure 9). Focusing on more limited areas for matrix development is essential for pragmatic reasons. In all but the smallest of institutions, the compilation of a comprehensive learning matrix would prove unmanageable unless there was a wall or two that needed permanent decorating.

The best approach is to have several different groups work on the subgroups and learning areas that have been designated as high-priority areas, thus creating a series of more detailed learning matrices.

Once a fairly comprehensive list of needs for a particular subgroup has been prepared, it should be reviewed by one or more instructors and perhaps by a student as well. Faculty members may suggest other items for inclusion or omission and indicate department priorities. Interaction between faculty members and librarians will graphically demonstrate the librarians' concern for curriculum planning and desire to support the faculty's own objectives. It may also expand the faculty's understanding of how much library-related learning their students should know. On the secondary and college levels it will not hurt to have a few advanced students review the matrix and pinpoint the most useful learning experiences at each level of specialization from their perspective.

One caution about learning needs: they are much more extensive than most librarians realize. For example, it simply is not sufficient to think that teaching new students how to use an index to periodicals will mean that they can retrieve needed information from the periodicals themselves. Depending on the size and complexities of the individual library, there may be a lot more to learn before the student can have a successful library experience. The process should be thought through step-by-step, lest the learning experience lack essential ingredients that the librarians have long since taken for granted. In this example, the steps would include:

GROUPS TO BE SERVED	LEARNING NEEDS	Orientation	Survival Skills	Locating Monographs	Locating Periodical Articles	Education Index	ERIC (manual)	ERIC (on-line)	Current Index to Journals in Education	Education Abstracts	Resources in Education
Undergraduate Students											
Academically Disadvantaged											
Beginning Students											
Beginning Majors											
Advanced Majors											
Graduate											
New to Campus											
Continuing from Undergraduate Programs											
Teaching Assistants											
Research Assistants											
Faculty											
New											
Full-time											
Part-time											

NOTE: Each learning need area would eventually be broken down further. For example, the term-paper skills would include a series of learning needs including how to use encyclopedias for gaining overviews on selected topics, how to take notes, how to organize the contents, how to make footnotes, etc. Likewise the introduction to the library might include learning where the basic service points are

Figure 9. Matrix for education students

Basic Reference Materials	Basic Education Reference Materials (e.g., *The Encyclopedia of Education, Education Yearbook, Yearbook of Higher Education*)	Specialized Education Reference Materials (e.g., guides to media materials, education in specific subject areas)	Curriculum Collection	Test File	Location of Education Materials in Area	State Government Documents on Education	Federal Government Documents on Education	Search Strategy	Term-Paper Skills	Etc.

located, how to secure a library card, how to check books out, how to obtain reserve materials, etc., as well as attitudinal learning concerning the value of the library to learning, the supportiveness of librarians, etc. See also the enumeration in the following text for the learning steps in securing a periodical article.

1. What index should be used?
2. How does one know which volume of the index to use?
3. What if an article is too recent to appear in a volume of the index?
4. How does one interpret the entries in the index?
5. How does one determine the name of the desired magazine from the abbreviation?
6. How much of the entry should be copied?
7. How many entries should be copied before proceeding?
8. How does one determine whether the library has a particular magazine?
9. How does one find the magazine?
10. How does one obtain it (fill out a slip, take it off a shelf)?
11. What if the magazine is missing or the article ripped out?
12. How does one determine if it is a "good" article?
13. How does one operate a microfilm reader? (How can one copy from it?)
14. How can one check out the magazine?
15. Where can one copy the article?
16. What can one do to obtain an article from a magazine the library does not have?
17. Why are there other indexes; how much does one need to know about them?
18. If one gets stuck, where is there help?

The affective domain, too, should be thought through in detail. What attitudes about libraries should users have, and what types of learning experiences can promote such attitudes? How people feel about libraries has more to do with how much they will use them than any other factor except specific class assignments. Surely, then, it is essential to judge the success of library instruction activities not only in terms of the way in which they fulfill cognitive learning objectives, but also in terms of their effect on basic attitudes. Success in the former area does not necessarily bring success in the latter. For example, it is now generally accepted among people experienced in library user-education programs that orientation tours early in the freshman year can be successful only if limited objectives in the affective domain are sought, whereas efforts to have students learn in any other area (e.g., how to use the card catalog or an index) as part of the tour are not only largely doomed to failure but will also have a negative effect on most students' attitudes toward the library. Learning matrices, therefore, must include attitudinal needs.

Public Libraries

For any public library to develop and maintain a successful program of user education, the planning process must include the identification of groups to be served, the establishment of priorities among them, and the determination of the groups' information-handling needs. The scope of the necessary considerations involved in this aspect of the planning is much broader for public libraries, but the process outlined for school and academic libraries is still appropriate.

While school and academic libraries have a wide spectrum of groups to serve, the groups they serve can be clearly identified and guidance in setting priorities is provided by institutional commitments. The public library, which has no built-in homogeneous clientele, is faced with a problem of quite a different magnitude when identifying target groups.

Recruitment is necessary for each public library instruction activity, and the number who respond usually cannot be predicted or controlled. Moreover, the participants in any one program will usually have a wide variety of library-use interests and represent a wide range of ages and levels of education.

Publicity is more crucial to the success of a library user-education program in a public library than in the school or academic setting. Publicity efforts almost become instruction activities in and of themselves, because in order to alert people to the instruction program, they must be made aware of their own needs.[2]

Obviously, no program can reach all members of the community. If data from a community analysis are available, they can be used, along with the librarians' firsthand knowledge of community priorities and concerns, their experience in dealing with library patrons, and their knowledge of community organizations, to make a determination of what groups can effectively be served.

One procedure is to establish a small planning committee made up of a few library employees to compile a list of potential groups of people to be served by the program. The committee should include librarians or others who can represent various segments of the community. At a staff meeting the list can be reviewed for additions, and a general discussion can be held regarding the perceived needs of various groups. After further consultation, the committee can then choose two or three of the groups to be served in the first cycle of the user-education program and submit their recommendations to the library director. To make it clear that the program is not ignoring nontargeted groups, care should be taken in communications with library board members and the general public to point out that this is only the first phase in the program and that inquiries and suggestions for future endeavors are welcome. Clearly, however, part of the decision on initial target populations has to be made on the basis of political considerations. In addition, public libraries, like school and academic libraries, must also give consideration to the needs of library employees for instruction.

If the range of groups to be served by public libraries is greater than those of other types of libraries, so also is the range of learning experiences needed. At one end of the spectrum there is the increasing number of people seeking to do in-depth study in a particular area without engaging in a formal educational program. Efforts such as the Adult Independent Learner Project have tried to address such needs.[3] At the other end is the increasingly acknowledged responsibility for public libraries to teach or facilitate the teaching of reading. At a meeting of the Pacific Northwest Library Association, the rationale for addressing literacy was succinctly summarized by one public librarian: "Our budgets and our continued existence depend upon the reading ability of our patrons and their continued interest in books and information materials."[4]

Library literacy programs are an essential aspect of user education. Literacy programs bring people to the library where resources at different reading levels and in different mediums are immediately accessible. With only a little imagination and planning, participants in the literacy program can be encouraged to become lifelong users of the library. To a large degree the particular library instruction needs of adults with low reading abilities parallel those of academically unprepared college freshmen, and literature dealing with each of these groups should be helpful to the other.

Between the library instruction needs of the barely literate adult and the adult seriously pursuing an independent learning project there are other groups to serve as well, ranging from the small businessman, the housewife who has just moved into the neighborhood, preschoolers, and the scores of schoolchildren who come to the library individually or in groups.

5. Setting Priorities

A serious exploration of user groups and their information-related learning needs will surely require consideration of a multiplicity of desirable activities. In order not to hamper creativity during the planning process, it is far better to consider users and their needs without worrying at the outset about the realities of current budgets and staffing. First be sure of the potential audiences for the instruction program, set priorities among them, and thoughtfully and comprehensively explore their learning needs. Then, once the whole matrix of needs is laid out, begin to admit the economic realities into the planning process.

After a planning group has had time to study the data that have been collected, a good brainstorming session can effectively list the instruction areas of greatest concern. The priority worksheet described in Chapter 3 should also be helpful.

Of course, if library skills tests were administered at regular intervals throughout elementary and high-school years, at entrance to college, and at the time students began their academic specialization, the learning needs of particular groups at various educational levels could be easily documented. Unfortunately, little such testing takes place, and such a determination is largely a subjective matter that depends upon the experience and sensitivity of librarians and, in some cases, classroom instructors. Moreover, no program of testing could produce all the information important to the determination of instruction priorities, because some considerations are political in nature. Normally, in making a determination of instruction priorities for a particular year the following factors must be considered:

1. Learning needs of the majority of people
2. Learning needs that are basic or fundamental

49

3. Learning needs in areas where there are already known supporters of user education
4. Existing programs that may be built or improved upon
5. Established (or opportunities for) requirements for library skills
6. Learning needs expressed by a group of people or documented through an evaluation process
7. Learning needs in highly visible programs or situations
8. Learning needs that relate to interests of influential people
9. Learning needs that clearly support priorities of the institution or community
10. Areas of great interest to library staff.

Once a priority list of instruction concerns has been completed, a review of the list may well lead to the elimination of those that are clearly less important. This revision is particularly important if the list is too long to be implemented.

The operational objectives that remain should be developed by using a standardized form (e.g., the one given in Figure 3 in Chapter 3). If the objectives have been prepared by different individuals, they should be reviewed by the entire planning group. If an objective is not clear enough to be stated precisely, or if no appropriate way to evaluate it can be thought of, the worksheet for that objective should be put aside for later consideration. If the rationale for adopting an objective does not relate to institutional commitments or compelling educational needs, it probably should also be put aside.

If everyone is in agreement that the remaining objectives are worthwhile and of more or less equal importance, the next step is to consider administrative limitations that might interfere with their successful completion. Such limitations fall under six general categories:

Limited financial resources
Limited human resources
Lack of skills
Lack of credentials/cooperation
Lack of facilities
Lack of time.

Financial and human resources can be redirected from other library operations only to a limited extent. No matter how worthwhile the objective, if the resources required cannot be located in advance, it should be postponed until they can be secured. In some cases an intermediate objective is required—i.e., to secure resources through grant sources.

The successful completion of many worthwhile objectives could also be jeopardized by lack of appropriate skills. Few librarians, for example, are trained in curriculum development, instructional methods, and/or audiovisual production. Some objectives may have to be postponed until librarians can acquire new skills or until other means of tapping the required expertise are identified. If relevant instructional materials can be purchased and adapted, some of these troubles can be circumvented.

As has already been noted in Chapter 2, academic librarians may sometimes encounter difficulties because they lack the credentials usually held by faculty. If faculty cooperation is necessary for the successful completion of a user-education objective, honest assessment of faculty attitudes toward librarians, especially their willingness to accept librarians as instructors, is necessary. Of course, there may be other reasons for lack of cooperation. The important thing is to be as sure as possible before adopting an objective that the necessary cooperation from people or offices outside the library will be forthcoming. For example, if access to ninth-grade students' grades is needed, can assurance be obtained that the grades will be made available? Can the library be sure that professors will require all their students to complete a library skills workbook as part of a course if this is necessary to the program? Whenever possible, such assurances of cooperation should be obtained in writing. If it is politically difficult to get written assurance, a memo from the library to those involved, reviewing the procedures agreed upon, will suffice. Obviously, having something in writing is no guarantee of cooperation; however, it does ensure that everyone clearly understands his or her responsibilities, has acknowledged them, and is therefore more likely to follow through.

Lack of suitable space for instruction within the library, lack of audiovisual facilities, or other physical plant and equipment limitations may also require the dropping or postponing of program objectives. Finally, even when the necessary talent and facilities are there, an objective might be so time-consuming or require such a long time for completion that it may be considered unfeasible. For example, if it is necessary that the user-education program accomplish something visible within six months, the very worthwhile objective of developing a major audiovisual, self-paced learning packet would have to be postponed in favor of another objective that would produce more immediate results.

Why not keep all these elements in mind while writing the initial program objectives, immediately eliminating those that involve administrative limitations? The reason is threefold. First, such foresight is not conducive to planning. If, instead of thinking about what should happen everyone is thinking about what cannot happen, much that is important to a quality program will be lost before it is ever begun. Second, if an objective is identified as really important, administrative limitations should not necessarily cause it to be dropped. Rather, creative thinking at its best is called for. What other approaches or resources can be utilized to overcome the initially perceived limitations? If there is no way around the limitations now, what can be done to ensure some solutions in the future? Third, circumstances do change. Highly desirable educational outcomes may be perceived before it is clear how they can possibly be implemented. It is important to identify the desired outcomes and the hindrances to their implementation, and to monitor these hindrances until an opportunity to move ahead occurs.

After this weeding-out process, the remaining program objectives should be looked at as a totality. Does it seem realistic to work on the remaining objectives all at once? If not, one or more may have to be postponed.

Once the total package seems reasonable, objectives should be developed in detail. Lists should be made of what activities will be undertaken in what order and within what time frame, the persons responsible, and the level at which each activity will occur.

This detailing of the program objectives serves two major purposes. First, it is the final check on their feasibility. As the activities, time frames, and personnel are specified, unexplored assumptions and overlooked difficulties will emerge as snags in the projected undertaking and, if unresolvable, will cause the objective to be rethought or dropped.

Second, the detailing serves as the operational guide for implementation. It spells out step-by-step what should take place. Therefore, it also serves as a check. Someone should be responsible for monitoring progress in implementation at predetermined intervals, for if activities are not being accomplished on time, a re-evaluation of the objective or at least a reconsideration of its timing should take place.

The completed program objectives should then be put in priority order, if possible, for presentation to the person or group of people authorized to adopt them as part of the library's public-service program for the coming year. It should thus be clear to everyone that the program objectives are not only important, but also possible. The remainder of the battle will consist of competing successfully with other worthwhile operational and program objectives from other areas of the library.

Nothing suggested in this book is more difficult in practice than setting priorities and eliminating worthwhile objectives. There are so many requests and opportunities for instruction, and there is so much enthusiasm among staff involved in the user-education programs that the deliberate elimination or postponement of identified areas of concern is extremely painful. The difficulty is roughly equivalent to the frustration of having to limit the contents of a particular learning experience. The admonition in both cases is the same: too little is better than too much. The librarian may despair over any lost opportunity to teach anything to anyone, but it is always better for instructors to present less, do it well, and ensure a successful learning experience. In the case of program adoption, it is preferable to undertake fewer objectives and activities, and to ensure that each is a successful, positive experience for all involved.

6. The Characteristics of Good Library Instruction

One of the best means to improve the quality of user-education programs is to apply the general principles of good instruction. The strong interrelationship of user-education programs and instruction in general were discussed in Chapter 1 where the use of library resources to support the over-all teaching quality of an educational institution was discussed.

The crucial element in all good teaching/learning experiences is the learners themselves. Because of conflicting demands on their time and energies, students develop coping strategies to maximize satisfaction and to minimize regrets. They are involved continually in assessing potential rewards and punishments and the probability of attaining various goals. If they do not have time to do all their assignments, they will do those which offer the best potential for achievement and may not do those which hold no threat if ignored. If library instruction carries no credit or is not seen to contribute directly to success in a course, it is at a considerable disadvantage. The demands of families and jobs exacerbate the situation. On the other hand, if students see value in the instruction for their courses, jobs, or homes, their motivation can significantly increase.

Fortunately, there is a great deal known about what motivates people, and most of it seems a matter of common sense. First, people are more likely to learn what they want to learn rather than what does not interest them. Students who are already interested in libraries or research will clearly benefit from a library instruction program. But for those—and there are many—who have had little experience with libraries, or whose experiences have been negative, particular efforts will be required.

Second, the attitude of the librarians can help set a positive tone by emphasizing the relevance of the instruction to the short- and long-term needs of the students. Librarians influence students in more subtle ways, too, by the impression they give about how they feel about their work, themselves, and their clients.

Third, the importance the classroom instructor places upon library instruction and library use has a strong influence on how students perceive library instruction. Faculty normally do not stress library use. Unless they are involved in research, most rely on discussions with colleagues and materials in their own collections for their own use, and on the library's reserve collections to meet the reading needs of their students. Students tend to replicate this pattern by conferring with fellow students and buying their own books to supplement the reserve materials. Therefore, the cultivation of faculty interest in and support for library instruction and the consequent contribution of classroom efforts will always be important in motivating students.

Fourth, people want to be liked. Both instructors and librarians have numerous opportunities to exhibit appreciation for students' library performances. Such little things as a word of praise or a written comment can go far toward building motivation. Studies in education have consistently shown that the performance of students given additional attention will improve more than that of those who did not receive such attention.[1]

Fifth, people are motivated by a desire to succeed, not to fail. Thus, it is important that the learning experience be structured to guarantee success. Computer-assisted instruction and programmed instruction, for example, work on this principle. Libraries can be overwhelming to the uninitiated. Every precaution must be taken to present their resources in manageable doses and in a logical framework, so that the learner can eventually pull the pieces together. Through reinforcement, students should come to understand that they can be successful users of the library.

Sixth, the closer the realization of goal or the greater the threat of not reaching it, the higher the motivation. This is one of the reasons why librarians have found that the most eager reception for library instruction comes when a research paper has been assigned.

Seventh, students' resentment of very close direction and contrary anxiety over independence also may motivate them toward library learning. The research paper is usually the best opportunity for independent study. Concerns about choosing a topic, how long to make the paper, what kind of paper the teacher really wants, combined with immediacy of the deadline, may lead to a perception of the library as a source of support. Librarians, however, must learn to walk that difficult line between too much direction and too much independence in structuring their instruction activities.

Library Users as Information Consumers

To build motivation for library instruction, it is most important to understand the learners' attitudes as information consumers. To them information is one of a multitude of goods. But although people generally want more goods, they tend to want less information. Whereas the typical librarian wants to help a person find *all* the information available on a topic, the average learner wants only that amount necessary to the problem or project at hand. The librarians' "overkill approach" at the reference desk and in instruction is hardly justifiable on intellectual grounds when one considers the obsolescence rate of information and the fact that a large number of searches *can* be satisfied by a small portion of the available sources. Overkill works against motivating students. Experience has shown that students simply do not remember what they do not have an immediate need to use, and an overexposure to library resources may overwhelm them and cause fearful and negative feelings toward the library.

Every attempt should be made to tie library instruction learning experiences directly to assignments. Drawing the line between "nice to know" and "essential" is not always easy, but it makes a big difference in student reception.[2] The reason is simple. All choices, including decisions about which information sources to use, involve costs in terms of time and effort—costs that must be spread over a wide variety of conflicting demands.

Different people place different values on information. It is therefore important to understand the value structure of the learners. It would probably not be far wrong to suggest that many students would not really be concerned about the accuracy of information presented in a class paper if the instructor was not concerned. (Consider the emphasis on many campuses on communication skills to the exclusion of concern for having something worth writing or talking about.) Furthermore, since the future is unsure for most students, they see learning about information resources and information-handling skills, whether in general or within a particular field, as of questionable value.

There are some students, of course, who are motivated by the sheer joy of accomplishment. Those students are frequently library users already and are excited about the discovery of new resources. Sometimes their enthusiasm can, by accident or design, have spillover on others. This effect is one of the principles involved in the concept of peer tutoring discussed in Chapter 11.

Further exploration is needed about how to motivate the learning of library-related skills and resources. At a 1973 British Conference, "The Education of Users of Scientific and Technical Information," this need was articulated:

> In exploring this field of *motivation* particular investigation should
> be made into the preferences of users in the way information is
> presented and what elements of future trends should be taken into
> account. Is it possible to discern a pattern of acceptability accord-
> ing to discipline, level or other variable and how far is what is
> acceptable removed from what is really needed?[3]

Librarians are aware of how resources vary from one field to another, e.g.,
the difference between the literatures for the fields of history and biology or
between a multidisciplinary area like gerontology and a specialized field
like linguistics. Given such variance, it is only logical that the presentation
formats and motivation levels should vary at particular points according to
discipline. Research is obviously needed in these areas, as user-education
programs in different disciplines are now amazingly similar.

The second key concept in how students acquire knowledge is the
organization of the learning experience. Three principles prevail:

1. Active learning is more effective than passive.
2. Learning should be as close to real-life situations as possible.
3. Practice works only if learners see results from their practice.

Active learning means engaging students' minds in thinking through a
process or problem. The ideal is to present a problem so important that
students are always thinking one step ahead of the instructor. The problem
with most lectures, whether in the classroom or from the pulpit, is that
people are talked to rather than being required to think through the issues
themselves. (The limitations of this process are evidenced by how quickly
Sunday morning sermons are forgotten.) On the other hand, if students are
each assigned a problem to research in the library before the librarian talks
with them, the discussion can grow out of their successes and failures. This
learning process is an intellectually engaging one.

Bringing the learning experience as close to real life as possible has two
chief advantages. First, it is easier for students to perceive the relationship
between what they are doing and what they want or need to do. Second,
such an approach helps students to develop habits and procedures that will
carry over into the other areas of their studies and eventually into their work
responsibilities. The real-life approach avoids a basic fault in most library
instruction. In real life people have an information need and approach the
library to meet that one specific need. In library instruction, far too often,
people are taught about basic types of resources and appropriate access tools;
thus, much library instruction resembles watered-down library school
courses. Learning search strategies is the real-life approach; it is the natural
core of mature user-education programs. Obviously, the real-life approach

is enhanced when there is an assignment due or when the public library patron has an immediate project in mind.

Practice by itself is not sufficient. Reaction is also essential. Almost everyone has had the experience of mispronouncing a word for years or performing some routine in a manner that was not as efficient or productive as possible until someone pointed out the correct or better way. The reaction not only precludes the continued practice of incorrect or inefficient procedures but also provides positive reinforcement as well. Reaction in the form of grades and spoken or written comments provides direction for further learning and motivation for increased learning. Immediate reaction is even better, as has been shown by the success of inexpensive latent-image technology in a library skills workbook at Lansing Community College in Michigan:

> Instant feedback increases learning, but it has had another effect that was not anticipated. The previous year we had used essentially the same workbook except that the answers were recorded on a machine scorable card. Students did not know until the completion of the workbook which questions they had answered correctly. Many students became discouraged. They either did not complete the score card at all, or at some point they began to randomly select answers. Approximately 20–25% of the students failed to complete the workbook: they simply gave up. The next year using essentially the same workbook except that this time it was in a format to provide instant feedback, fewer than 5% of the students gave up. Instant feedback provides the positive reinforcement students need to complete the workbook. This undoubtedly influences their feelings about the workbook assignment, and thus their feelings about the library itself.[4]

Active learning, real-life learning, and reaction are summed up in the concept of learning by discovery. This term refers to learning situations in which students develop generalizations from specific instances in varying contexts.[5] It is the very manner of experiential learning by which children become acquainted with their environments and begin to find meaning in it. Moreover, it is an active process that involves practice that is constantly being modified through feedback. Library instruction activities that are organized to provide learning by discovery will have moved a long way toward ensuring success. Indeed, allowing students to discover principles may enhance motivation, the other necessary ingredient to successful learning experiences.

Growing out of the motivation and organization concerns supporting quality teaching/learning experiences and based upon the experiences of many librarians, a set of seven guidelines can be constructed to characterize good library instruction.

Characteristics of Good Library Instruction

Library instruction should be people oriented; it should begin with people's needs and concentrate on processes and search strategies rather than focusing on library tools or resources.

Library instruction should provide student-centered learning. Since students vary in their preferred style of learning and speed of learning, alternative learning experiences should be provided.

After every learning experience students should be able to *do* something and to have confidence that they can do it.

Too little in a learning experience is better than too much.

AV materials should be used to intensify positive learning experiences.

Library instruction should remain flexible.

Library instruction should be evaluated.

A few other dos and don'ts should be mentioned in the interests of promoting quality library instruction. The first concerns terminology. Some librarians feel that no concessions should be made in the use of nonprofessional terms in teaching library skills and resources. They argue that if people are going to use libraries, they will have to learn library terminology sooner or later. The problem is that such unwillingness to sidestep jargon imposes another learning experience on top of the primary one. This attitude is a disservice to the learner. The extra baggage is almost always unnecessary to achieving the stated learning objectives and should be eliminated on that basis alone. (Chapter 7 will elaborate this point.) Librarians should teach professional terms only when absolutely necessary.

Unnecessary instruction is another danger. Years ago, Branscomb warned that "unnecessary instruction is deadly for the student and expensive for the institutions, and that students vary greatly in their need for [library instruction]."[6] As more planning undergirds user-education programs, there should be fewer occasions for unnecessary repetition of learning experiences by requiring people to participate who have, in one way or another, already mastered the material. Whenever there is some way of documenting competency or serious reason to anticipate that some people will already be knowledgeable, those learners should be separated and channelled into more advanced work or into supporting the learning processes of others. Good library instruction will always be flexible enough to accommodate a range in ability and provide a means for exemption. (This question is dealt with more extensively in Chapter 10.)

Finally, differences in preferred learning styles suggest that good library instruction will be structured to allow for such diversity. Particularly in the areas of widespread learning needs, more than one learning experience should be available. Thus, lectures, point-of-use materials, and self-paced workbooks might all be available as a means of learning how to use ERIC materials. These opportunities would allow people to consider their schedules, what their friends are doing, or simply which approach appeals to them the most in choosing how to cover the material. Such variety also provides backup for those learners who have more difficulty than others in mastering specific material. For example, a lecture can be reinforced by experience with a point-of-use AV package. The backup is also useful when learners miss a scheduled activity since time-consuming individualized makeup work is no longer necessary.

Good library instruction comes much more from careful planning than from natural talent. This observation should be a comfort to most librarians who never expected to be teachers. The emphasis should always be on the learning rather than on the teaching. Librarians should appear to be facilitators of learning within programs of user education just as they have always been facilitators of learning in fulfilling their reference responsibilities. The challenge is to know enough about what factors make for good teaching/learning experiences and to do enough planning to ensure quality library instruction.

7. Setting Instructional Objectives

Many may ask if it is really necessary to set instructional objectives. Surely, if one is clear on the materials that should be covered and presents them in a logical and lively way, that should be enough. This is a tempting approach to take because objective-setting, like most new skills, is not easily mastered and can be quite frustrating at first. There are, however, several important reasons why it is necessary.

Objective-setting is first and foremost a discipline; it forces one to think in terms of desired learner outcomes. Good library instruction should start with the needs of users and be learner-centered throughout; yet this approach is contrary to librarians' natural tendencies. From library school on, they are taught to think in terms of categories of resources and the organization of information. Writing instructional objectives addresses this problem. It disciplines the librarian to think of the desired end results: what is it that the student should be capable of doing after the learning experience? It allows the librarian and the student to know when the learning has been completed, since instructional objectives state what action signifies accomplishment. Good objectives also spell out how success will be measured; they allow the librarian and student to know not only when the learning has been accomplished but also how well.

Focusing on desired outcomes in terms of student performance disciplines the planner in another manner as well. The single most frequent mistake in library instruction is trying to squeeze as much information as possible into a given teaching/learning experience. The motivation is noble. The librarian is not sure that the students will have another exposure to library instruction. There is so much that it would be advantageous for students to know that the impulse to mention one other source, one more

61

index, one more reference book, etc., is impossible to resist. After all it is for the "good" of the students.

But, as we have stated in Chapter 6, in fact, such overkill is *not* for the good of the students. Past a certain point, the more information presented, the more likely it is that students will remember less. It is better to cover less so that students can absorb the information presented and feel confident that they can follow through on the opportunities it presents in exploiting library resources, rather than to leave them with a bewildered confusion. An instructional objective provides the measuring stick by which to determine what contents should be included in the learning experience, for anything that does not directly support accomplishment of an objective should not be included.

Writing instructional objectives is also a foundation for teaching. *After* the objective is written, the methodology and the contents are chosen. Too many librarians begin with a methodology and force all contents into it. How many campuses, for example, confine their instruction activities almost exclusively to workbooks or course offerings? Good instruction is close to real life. Therefore, only after the desired learner outcome is determined can a learning process be chosen for the particular group of students involved. Setting objectives first encourages the examination of alternative approaches to mastering the same material. It also opens up the door to the use of multiple approaches to the learning of the same material—a state that is heartily to be desired given the diversity of the people libraries serve.

Setting instructional objectives can also serve as an important communication link with instructors. If the objectives are developed within the framework of the goals of an academic department, they can clearly demonstrate how library instruction will support the student achievement that the department wants. In effect the librarian becomes a partner in the educational process.

At the same time, instructional objectives help students to see how library instruction relates to their primary areas of concern, and to organize themselves to accomplish the stated objectives. Students begin to work—both consciously and unconsciously—toward the accomplishment of the instructional objectives once they know them and perceive that they have a meaningful relationship to their concerns.

In summary, instructional objective-setting is necessary to quality programs of library instruction, because it:

> Demands disciplined thinking in terms of learner outcomes
> Is the foundation process from which methodologies, contents, and evaluative procedures are chosen

Effectively limits program content

Serves as a communication link with faculty

Helps students to organize themselves to accomplish stated learning outcomes.

Librarians who have no experience in setting instructional objectives, or who need to brush up on the topic, should see Robert F. Mager's *Preparing Instructional Objectives*,[1] a self-paced learning experience that can easily be gone through in one evening. It will give the librarian a conceptual understanding of the elements of good instructional objectives, as well as some experience in working with them. Sample objectives in this chapter will supplement Mager's examples by emphasizing a library perspective.

Two sources on objective writing for library instruction place this process within the context of broader program planning, give concrete guidelines for writing objectives, and suggest forms for facilitating the process. One, *Developing Objectives for Library Instruction*,[2] is by Jacquelyn M. Morris and by Donald F. Webster; the other, "A Scientific Model for the Development of Library Use Instruction Programs,"[3] is a paper by Marvin E. Wiggins. Their terminology and some details differ, but their approaches are similar to those of this book.

Mager, in particular, keeps jargon to a minimum and takes a common-sense approach to the whole process of objective-setting. His practical, down-to-earth approach is surely the right one for librarians. In its simplest terms, an instructional objective is a description of a performance the instructor wants learners to be able to exhibit. It is a statement of the intended result of the instruction.

The basic and necessary element of every instructional objective is the performance statement. It indicates what the learner is expected to be able to do after the instruction. There are two types of performances. Overt performances are those that consist of observable actions. For example, if the desired outcome is that students will be able to identify and locate books on needed topics, the instruction's contents might be the card catalog, the L.C. classification system, the stack arrangement, and the procedures for checking out a book. But the objective will read:

> Students will check out books on predetermined topics.

Other objectives deal with covert performances, i.e., those that are concerned with abstractions or attitudes. Such an objective might focus on students' understanding of the purpose of the reference desk. The objective could be:

> Students will know that the reference desk is where one goes for information.

Unfortunately, one cannot see the inner workings of students' minds and so cannot "see" what students do or do not know. Thus, in preparing an objective for a covert performance, while it is important to state the main intent of the objective, it is always necessary to add a statement on student behavior or action that will indicate the existence of the abstraction or attitude. If, for example, students can be observed actually going to the reference desk for information, their action can be accepted as an outward indication that they have internalized the fact that the reference desk is the place to go for information. The objective might read:

> Students will evidence understanding that the reference desk is where one goes for information by picking up the orientation packet, which was explained in the class session.

A second element of most instructional objectives is an indication of the level at which the concept or skill should be mastered before the objective is considered accomplished and the student can move ahead. Criteria deal with such matters as accuracy, speed, and quality. At this point, the following criterion might be added:

> Ninety percent of the students will evidence understanding that the reference desk is where one goes for information by picking up the orientation packet, which was explained in the class session, from the reference desk.

Using the earlier example, the following criterion might be added:

> Students will check out five books on the topics chosen for their English 102 papers.

In this case there are two criteria for success: the number of books specified and the requirement that the books be suitable for a specific class assignment. (The suitability might need further specification, such as acceptability to the English 102 instructor.) In both examples given, speed is not of primary importance and so is not included. However, in an instructional objective concerned with library employees mastering filing rules, time as well as accuracy might be stated criteria:

> Within fifteen minutes the employee will file the set of book cards with 95 percent accuracy.

These criteria can be objectively measured, in contrast to the suitability of the books to the chosen topic in the prior example, which is of a more subjective nature. In some cases the criterion might point to available checklists, guidelines, or examples. Examples of criteria of this type are:

> Footnotes will be prepared according to Turabian.

or

The student will footnote the research paper according to the following examples:

Book

1. Kenneth Walton, *The Rise and Fall of a Boy* (New York: Happy Publishers, 1980), p. 16.

Periodical article

1. Kenneth Walton, "Unicorns I Have Known," *Star Fleet Chronicles* 1:16 (Apr. 18, 1964).

The final element in some instructional objectives is a statement of conditions. Conditions specify what may be required, allowed, or restricted, whether the use of certain skills or tools is to be permitted, or what other conditions affect performances. Conditions should not be added unless necessary. Examples of conditions would be:

Without using the *Reader's Guide*, students will locate three articles which will be used in their assigned English 102 papers.

or

Using *Education Index*, students will locate three articles which will be used in their assigned Education 201 paper.

In the first example use of one tool is excluded; in the second, use of a particular tool is required. In one case the condition demands learning beyond the most basic of indexes and in the other, the use of one particular index. Obviously, the contents chosen for the two learning experiences will vary considerably.

Some general guidelines are worth underscoring. First, until one is well experienced in writing objectives, it is best to work in a small group. Brainstorming can be extremely helpful in reaching that precise combination of words that will clearly indicate the desired learning outcome to the learner, the faculty member, and the librarian. Keep the objective as simple as possible; use as few words as possible. Never add a condition unless it is necessary to the intent of the instruction. Check for ambiguous words and be particularly careful of verbs. (Mager lists good and bad verbs.) Using a blackboard when developing objectives helps the playing around with words that is an intrinsic part of writing instructional objectives.

Whenever possible, share a next-to-final draft of objective(s) with the faculty member concerned and with some students. Make sure that the intent of an objective is as clear to them as it is to those who developed it. This procedure has the added advantage of further educating faculty about how the library is supporting their own instructional efforts. On the other hand, if the objectives do not fit the instructor's plans, far better to know it before students receive the library instruction so that the objectives can be adjusted accordingly.

The sample objectives of this chapter may appear too simple at first glance to a librarian. In reality they provide all the guidance necessary for the next two steps in instructional development, choosing the methodology for the learning/teaching experience and choosing the contents. In the last example, nothing should be included that will not directly contribute to the ability of students to locate articles on a specific topic in the *Education Index*. Moreover, the objective is a straightforward and clear statement to the students and the instructor of what the students will have accomplished after completing the learning experience. Ideally, it will also document the library instruction component as one necessary element in the achievement of the broader objectives of the course.

8. Methodologies for Quality Instruction

Once a learning objective has been clearly stated, it is time to think about the kinds of experiences that will best facilitate it. Most objectives can be achieved through a number of different learning experiences. The approach to be taken, i.e., the methodology, should be determined on the basis of:

> Known administrative limitations (*see* Chapter 5)
> Potential for providing a quality learning experience
>> number of anticipated learners
>> involvement time available to the learner
>> extent to which learning needs relate to a specific project
>> or assignment
>> depth of learning required
> Flexibility
> Compatibility with abilities and interests of instructor.

Many methodologies can be quickly discarded simply because resources, facilities, or cooperation from outside the library are unavailable. After the elimination of clearly unfeasible methodologies, a number of approaches will in most cases still be possible. The final choice must then be made on the basis of which methodology (1) can best provide a quality learning experience; (2) will provide the most flexibility; and (3) best matches the abilities and interests of the librarian or other designated instructor.

No one methodology is necessarily better than another, and no one approach is more effective. Although individuals prefer varying learning styles, in normal group situations such differences average out. Only when dealing with groups that have some major limitation in common can any one or any subset of methodologies be clearly better than or inferior to others. For example, for a group with very low reading ability, no methodology should be chosen which requires heavy reading or writing. Public library clientele from the business community and part-time students with full-time jobs are obvious candidates for learning methodologies that fit into a flexible time schedule.

Four factors will affect the choice of methodology. The most important is the number of learners involved. If a maximum of 30 people is to be involved, the investment of time and resources to produce a self-paced multimedia package could not be justified, even though an excellent learning experience might result. An in-depth, two-day workshop conducted by a librarian in conjunction with a required course might be ideal unless 80 sections of the course need the workshop each semester and there is only one librarian to do all of the instruction. Obviously, the decision is also affected by whether the learners come in concentrated groups or are spread out. A self-paced audio and print tour might be ideal for a library that has many individuals requesting directional information.

The second most important factor in choosing a methodology is the time available to the learner. Ideally, the time available would be equal to the time needed to master the objective. In most cases, however, there is some externally imposed limitation. A specific length of time may be allotted for the program of a church or social group meeting held at the public library, or a fifty-minute class session may be scheduled in the school or academic library setting. Designated time frames may well require the elimination of promising methodologies. The time available, of course, clearly limits the amount of material that can be covered.

The other factors affecting the methodology relate to the purpose behind the learning experience. Approaches must be appropriate to the field of study, if the instruction is related to a class assignment or an independent learning project. Moreover, the methodology will depend on whether the learning required is on an introductory or a narrowly focused, in-depth level.

In choosing methodologies, one should also consider which ones can meet the needs of a variety of groups or can be easily modified for other subject areas. An indexed collection of transparencies can be used as an instructional aid for group presentations as well as for highlighting tools and processes during library tours. A point-of-use learning package can be used both by independent learners and as backup to a group lecture for those who learn more slowly or who are absent when the lecture is given. Such flexibility also allows for differences in preferred learning styles among learners and thus upgrades the entire library user-education program. The need for constantly updating information is another reason why flexibility is essential. In general, slides are preferable to films and looseleaf sheets to handbooks.

The particular talents and interests of the librarians or the instructors who will be developing or facilitating the learning experience affect methodology, too. Yet such factors should be considered only when two or more methodologies or combinations of methodologies seem to hold relatively equal potential for producing quality learning experiences. First, the learning objective is determined, then the potential of various methodologies to facilitate the achievement of the objective is evaluated, and finally, if choices still remain, the predilections of the individual instructor can determine the methodology finally chosen. To proceed in the opposite direction is to place the emphasis on the means rather than on the end.

An understanding of the strengths and weaknesses of the various methodologies can also help in choosing the best one for any given situation. In the chart given in Figure 10, methodologies for library instruction are compared with the qualities of good instruction cited in Chapter 6. The ratings represent an attempt to quantify the attitudes of a group of librarians with regard to a variety of typical learning situations. Certainly in evaluating or rating the approaches used within a particular library, the ratings would vary. The chart should serve as a useful model, however.

Several things are clear from the chart. First, no methodology is perfect. The group tour, still one of the most common methods of instruction, does not meet the criteria for quality library instruction. Grouping or combining two or more methodologies can provide for a better learning experience and thus facilitate the achievement of the stated learning objectives. Lectures can be complemented by instructional aids, handouts, and a follow-up lab experience. Brief AV productions geared to making students feel unthreatened in their first approach to the library, followed by a self-guided tour, can provide a more positive first experience in the library than either approach could provide separately, and good signage can further complement the orientation process.

In general, it is a good practice to identify two or more possible methodologies (or combinations of methodologies) for each stated objective. This practice will help to ensure that the final choice is made on the basis of the potential of the methodology for facilitating the accomplishment of the objective. Too frequently, the first methodology that comes to mind is the one with which the librarian is naturally most comfortable or the one that is traditionally taken. The exercise of listing alternative possibilities forces more creative thinking, which should be conducive to a

QUALITIES OF GOOD INSTRUCTION	Group Tour	Self-Paced Tour	Classroom Lecture	Library Lecture	Credit Course	Noncredit Course	Lab	Handouts	Signage	Displays	Point-of-Use	AV Production (For Group Viewing)	Instructional Aids	Workbooks	Programmed Instruction	Computer-Assisted Instruction	Term Paper Clinics	Combination
People oriented	0	0	½	½	½	½	½	½	½	0	+	½	½	½	½	½	+	+
Resembles real-life situations	0	0	0	0	½	½	+	0	0	0	+	0	0	½	½	½	½	+
Provides flexibility in learning approach or pace	0	+	0	0	½	½	½	+	+	+	+	0	0	+	+	+	0	+
Requires active involvement of learner	0	0	0	0	+	+	+	0	0	0	+	0	½	+	+	+	+	+
Carries built-in motivation	0	0	½	½	+	½	½	0	0	0	+	0	0	½	+	+	+	+
Concentrates on process or strategies	0	0	½	½	½	½	+	½	0	0	+	0	½	½	½	½	½	+
Encourages learner to do something after learning experience	0	0	½	½	+	+	+	½	½	0	+	0	½	+	+	+	+	+

+ = Methodology highly reflects the quality.
½ = Methodology sometimes can reflect quality.
0 = Methodology never or almost never reflects quality.

Figure 10. Comparison of library instruction methodologies

flexible and dynamic user-education program that is truly responsive to user needs. For example, consider the following objective taken from Chapter 7 and the possible methodologies to facilitate it:

Objective:
Using *Education Index*, students will locate three articles which will be used in their assigned Education 201 paper.
Possible methodologies:
1. Point-of-use: audiotape/sample page
2. Lecture with instructional aids and handouts
3. Workbook unit (programmed instruction)

The balance of this chapter will review methods of library instruction and highlight their strengths and weaknesses. The methodologies covered are those presented in Figure 10, with the exception of signs and displays which will be discussed in Chapter 12.

Tours

There are two major types of tours: those in which groups are shepherded by library staff and those that are self-conducted. On-the-screen tours are also often used to save staff time and to avoid having groups disturb readers and researchers working in the library.

Discussions with librarians from various sizes and types of libraries have revealed group tours to be of little value despite their widespread use. Tours do not help to accomplish most learning objectives. Indeed, group tours are on the bottom of the list when the qualities of good instruction are rated. Audiovisual productions, which largely duplicate what a walking tour would do, share these limitations and are often difficult to transfer to an actual library setting.

Group tours can, however, show librarians as helpful, friendly people who can help people to overcome initial hesitations about using the library. An effective tour developed in response to such affective learning objectives will however, omit mini-lectures on how to use the card catalog and indexes, and the dozens of other details normally crowded into orientation presentations. A brief audiovisual presentation may be as effective as a physical tour, without suffering from the disadvantages already mentioned. However, the learning experience would be greatly enhanced if there was some way to ensure that the presentation could be reinforced by the students' using the library soon afterward.

Self-guided tours do not require ongoing staff commitments, and they do allow complete flexibility in timing. Mini-tours can focus on just one service or resource area, rather than on providing a general over-all orientation to the library. A successful over-all exposure was developed by a faculty member at the University of Delaware for graduate students in the biosciences. The simple mimeographed guides plus supplementary printed materials (including a map) were deemed successful on two grounds: (1) they shifted the responsibility for learning from the staff to the individual students; and (2) students required less help in subsequently locating materials than they had in former years, when group tours were offered.[1] Self-guided tours require good signage. They can make good use of tape cassettes.

Lectures

Lectures are another very popular method of library instruction. The relative value of giving the lecture in the library as opposed to the classroom is in question. If the library has adequate facilities, bringing the students into it provides assurance that they will know where it is and makes it unnecessary to cart materials to classrooms. On the other hand, dealing with the students in their usual learning environment has some advantages, too. In either location, the presence of the classroom teacher is known to increase the importance that most students ascribe to the learning experience; dialogue between teacher and librarian enhances this effect.

In 1975 a study reported the opinions of 112 academic librarians about the role of classroom lectures, generally given at the invitation of instructors, in developing library skills needed for an assignment. The composite list of limitations cited in the study is lengthy. Some of these limitations, however, can be controlled, to some degree, by the efforts of librarians.

> Ranked in order of importance, these limitations were reported: lectures do not reach all students needing instruction; students encounter too much material in one session; the sources discussed are not handled or used until a later date; lectures cannot always be related to specific classroom needs; students do not see the value of the presentation; insufficient time is allotted for the presentation; and students assume the library can be mastered through the library lecture. These other disadvantages could be included: students do not like the lecture method; groups are often too large and this minimizes interaction; instructors assume that too much can be accomplished in one session; instructors assume

that lectures can be given without advance preparation or on short notice; material cannot always be made relevant and interesting; lectures can come too early in the term; sometimes only part of the class appears interested; and lectures may be repetitious of previous lectures, instruction, or knowledge.[2]

Of the fifteen concerns listed the only two which are inherent weaknesses in the lecture method are that students do not like the lecture method and that the sources discussed are not handled or used until a later date. Eight items deal with the need to develop better faculty support and cooperation; they include the need to motivate students better, a feat more easily accomplished by the classroom instructor than the librarian. Two areas are in control of the librarian: the amount of material presented and the material's interest and relevance. Relevance depends to some extent on the classroom instructor. Making material interesting depends on the librarian. The fact that not all students can be reached through lectures is not unique to this type of instruction, nor is the problem of repetition. If librarians can develop and strengthen working ties with faculty, the lecture method can be an effective methodology.

However, without careful planning lectures can be only minimally effective. Efforts to get students actively involved in thinking through search strategies and to get them to see the benefits of the material presented (e.g., having an assigned paper or speech) are important. The use of instructional aids to underscore key points, handouts to cover logistics (e.g., hours of the library), and pathfinders or guides to the library can enhance the lecture method. Combining the lecture with work in a library laboratory-type situation can be particularly effective if the librarian is available for consultation. Point-of-use materials can prove invaluable as backups to lectures for the learner who missed the session or who needs to go over the material again.

With adequate support mechanisms the lecture method can be a positive learning experience for people connected with all types of libraries. The problems cited which are unique to the academic or school setting can often be solved by developing strong cooperative relationships with classroom instructors.

Courses

In the academic setting, courses for credit have a particular allure for some librarians, perhaps because they enhance their feeling of being faculty members. Moreover, a credit course ensures enough time to cover needed materials. As attractive as this approach to library instruction may be, it is fraught with difficulties.

First, it is extremely time-consuming. It is no accident that an average faculty teaching load runs between 9 and 12 credits per semester. For the conscientious faculty member, the amount of time spent in preparing for the courses, evaluating student performance, advising, and pursuing research brings the work week within the 40- to 50-hour range. There are no real shortcuts to quality teaching; offering a full course will inevitably take considerable time from other activities in which librarians are involved. This is time that could undoubtedly be more profitably invested.

Second, there is the problem of motivation. It is difficult to relate library instruction to the immediate needs of the students, nor are classroom faculty present to support and endorse the need for research skills. If there is not the inducement of earning credits, the burden for motivating students rests entirely on the ability of the librarian to convince them (and to keep them convinced) that research skills are important. Moreover, even courses with credit are, generally, open electives; the result is that the students who choose them have very diverse abilities and interests, a further complication for the learning/teaching situation.

Whether or not credit is offered, the course may have visibility problems, which can only be solved by developing strong cooperative relationships with classroom instructors. Even if the course is cross-listed in the schedule under various academic programs, faculty will rarely promote it unless a good deal of preliminary public relations work has been done.

If credit is offered, the library finds itself competing for limited student hours. If the credits are offered directly by the library, the course is in competition with all academic programs (the competition increases as enrollment declines). If the credits are offered by one academic department, the course may be inappropriately identified with that department. If enrollment drops in the department, faculty support for a course offered by the library may disappear.

The one good solution is to have specialized courses within the curricula of different disciplines. Courses such as Business Sources of Information and Research Methods or Legal Research and Writing can be taught by a professor from the department, a librarian, or both, as a team. In this case the course is clearly part of the curriculum, and there is no sense of competition with the academic programs. Students will be a reasonably homogeneous group. A basis for motivation exists when such courses are required for graduation. In this way the librarian will be easily discerned as supporting the academic department's objectives, and students will have a substantial and positive experience and a clear understanding of how librarians can support their academic and professional or business efforts. And—perhaps most important—there will be ample time to cover the material.

Wherever possible, the library should be reimbursed for having its staff teach, or else librarians should teach such courses on an overload basis. The reason for this is very practical: if too many librarians are teaching such courses out of their "library time," over-all library operations will suffer. If enough courses are taught with financial reimbursement to the library, another librarian can be hired, or student hours in the library can be increased. Another approach might be to "trade" faculty. Can someone from the School of Education have release time to help produce instructional aids for the library? Can a professor have release time to help in collection development?

Laboratories

The laboratory approach to learning has long been accepted, particularly in the sciences. The need for hands-on or practicum experiences is also evidenced by the number of practice-teaching experiences, field experiences, and internships required or recommended by various academic programs. Such experiences provide students with an opportunity to put into practice the concepts they have been learning. Moreover, encountering problems in real-life situations can help students to identify weaknesses and may also increase motivation as students experience firsthand the value of the material covered at school.

Certainly the lab experience has a place in user-education programs. Until people actually use libraries and their resources, it is impossible for them to master search techniques or information-handling skills. Moreover, some repeated practice is necessary for retention.

The most ideal lab situation is the library itself, where the materials can be used directly. Having the librarian (and, in an educational institution, the classroom instructor) immediately available as a troubleshooter and as a monitor of progress is also important. Practical outcomes are an important part of establishing motivation. Learning will be reinforced if the students can use their newly discovered information on an assignment or on a project of interest to them.

Lab situations are almost always built into larger learning experiences and can also be used to break up sessions into periods compatible with interest spans. A derivative of the practice lab is to have learners try to find information on a specified subject before or at the beginning of a library instruction session.

Handouts

Most libraries produce handouts, ranging from floor plans of the library to extensive bibliographies, from information on library hours and services to guides or pathfinders to materials in particular subject areas. In recent years there has been a noticeable decline in the production of library handbooks that attempt to provide over-all, albeit superficial, coverage of the library and its resources. At the same time more guide sheets have been produced which can be used individually or can be combined in a folder to substitute for a handbook. The reasons for the shift include the ease with which information can be updated, lower costs, and greater flexibility. As long as the sheets are compatible in format and style, they can be an attractive and serviceable alternative to the handbook. Libraries (including public libraries) that need the more complete format, however, will do well to consult the standards for student and faculty handbooks produced by the Committee on Instruction and Use, Junior College Libraries Section, Association of College and Research Libraries.[3]

Handouts provide the most efficient and cost-effective means of transmitting large amounts of factual information. There is no reason why patrons should have to write down information on library hours or circulation rules during an orientation session. Why should valuable and limited learning time be spent on such details? Far better to concentrate on creating positive relationships or in helping patrons develop search strategies.

All handouts of a single library should be compatible in style and format. Guidelines in these areas should be developed and carefully followed. To accommodate standard paper size, handouts should be 8½-by-11 inches or 4¼-by-5½. Handouts should be dated and the chief author should be indicated. Someone should have responsibility for regularly reviewing them for adequate supply, accuracy, and currency. They should be easy for patrons to pick up and should also be incorporated appropriately into library instruction activities. New faculty and administrators should receive a basic package of handouts with a note of welcome from a librarian.

Pathfinders, which outline basic search procedures, are preferable to bibliographies, which by their nature are one-dimensional and quickly outdated. Pathfinders will direct patrons to all types of information on a particular subject by listing subject headings for the catalog, suggesting the best indexes and abstracts, and noting on-line data-base possibilities, appropriate government document series, pamphlet file headings, etc. Pathfinders should provide concrete guidance on how to structure a literature search. They should always suggest approaching a librarian for additional assistance if needed. Since pathfinders are instructional materials, thought should be given to including a brief evaluation form.

Point-of-Use

Point-of-use instruction can range from simple laminated instruction sheets to complex media packages. The term applies to all materials designed to teach patrons the use of library tools at the location of the tool itself.

From the users' perspective, point-of-use materials serve a number of specific purposes. They offer beginning information for patrons who are reluctant to ask for help and provide immediate instruction when otherwise there might be a wait for assistance. They may be gone over as frequently as desired without the feeling that one is being a burden or a nuisance to the librarian. They may be used as a backup to a library lecture. Most important, they can be consulted exactly when needed and when convenient. They offer the right instruction at the right time.

Point-of-use materials are often hailed as time-saving for library staff. This may or may not be true. First, there is a great deal of lead time required to produce such materials. If they are not done well, librarians may spend as much or more time explaining them to patrons as they would in directly teaching how to use the reference tools. Moreover, in today's world of sophisticated communications, people are accustomed to high-quality productions, and poor materials will not only fail to interest people but will have a negative effect on the total image of the library.

Care in choosing equipment is also very important. Nothing can be more harmful to developing a viable media program than undependable equipment. Besides durability, ease of repair, quietness of operation, and cost, it is necessary to take user preference into account. For example, telephone receivers are preferable to headsets. Before investment in equipment, discussion of options with libraries that offer similar programs or with a knowledgeable media person is valuable.

The Thomas Cooper Library at the University of South Carolina and the Barker Engineering Library at Massachusetts Institute of Technology have made extensive studies of point-of-use materials. These materials have been seen as part of the larger instruction program, and serious concern has been given to evaluating them either by self-tests or user questionnaires. At the Cooper Library one of the lessons learned over a number of years was that "no matter how intriguing the audiovisual programs may be, simple printed directions are sometimes not only sufficient but more effective."[4] Similarly, at the Barker Engineering Library, users preferred audio/sample-page programs to slide/tape.[5] As has already been underscored, it is important to match the methodology to the learning objective; likewise it is important to choose the right medium within the methodology. As often as not, a simpler medium will work as well as, or better than, a more sophisticated one. Since, for example, the sample page is more real-to-life than a set of slides, it provides a more positive learning experience while at the same time being easier and less expensive to develop.

Point-of-use materials require ongoing support if they are to be successful elements in the library user-education program. Not only are there initial production and purchase costs and ongoing maintenance costs, but there is also the cost of evaluating and updating the materials. Changes in the library, changes in the reference tools presented, and changing learner needs will all dictate revisions.

AV Productions for Group Viewing

In general, the best use of AV productions for group viewing is for general orientation and building positive attitudes toward the library and librarians. Stressing the importance of information in today's society, describing the ways in which libraries serve to make information available, or giving a brief introduction to a particular library or library service may offer appropriate focuses. The section on tours has noted the inherent dangers of including too much detailed information in such orientations. Concerns about production quality are even more serious in group AV presentations than point of use, since the potential for affecting attitudes is so great. Moreover, the larger screen makes mistakes and lack of quality all the more noticeable, not to mention the mounting negative effect that disenchanted or amused audience reactions can have. For these reasons, ongoing user evaluation and frequent updating are crucial. Some media lend themselves better to updating than others: slides are usually preferable to videotapes or films because of flexibility, cost, and ease of production.[6]

Audiovisual productions can serve a variety of functions. The Marriott Library at the University of Utah produced an excellent series of very short, high-quality, color videotapes about library services, such as interlibrary loan. Similar to advertisements on commercial television, each segment "sells" a single service, and the effectiveness of the selling in turn "sells" the library.

Where closed-circuit or cable-television opportunities exist and large numbers of people must be reached by the instruction program, thought should be given to the use of television for outreach. A number of tests have shown that television instruction, whether in library user-education programs or in other fields, is as effective as lectures or some other traditional approaches. Yet preparation demands far more work than is needed for developing lectures. The real advantage is in the numbers that can be reached and in the opportunity for successful orientation and strong image-building. Perhaps public libraries have made the best use of these possibilities to date. The public library in Amherst, New York, has for years produced a series of programs in which local dignitaries highlight a particular topic of interest to them and the librarian displays library materials on the subject. Not only is there a noticeable increase in the checking out of the materials discussed, but the library has developed an increasing support base made up of the dignitaries who were on the shows. Libraries of all types will do well to monitor developing television opportunities in their areas and to explore the potential they hold for user-education programs.

Instructional Aids

Everyone is familiar with the use of transparencies and slides in the classroom setting, and it is surprising that more librarians do not make use of such materials in their talks to groups. A good visual can clarify the points being made and help to ensure that everyone is focusing on the same point at the same time. Good visuals can also help to highlight the organization of a presentation and to emphasize main points. Learning experiences that involve more than one sense have higher retention rates; e.g., other things being equal, if people see a diagram of a search strategy in addition to hearing about it, they will remember it longer.[7] On the other hand, poor visuals are worse than no visuals at all for both the learning experiences and the image of the library.

Transparencies, large dummy cards, or slides can be helpful aids in discussions of catalog and index entries. How often has a librarian pulled out a catalog drawer and, by way of illustration, pointed to the heading on a card which could only be seen by those few standing close by? There is no reason why most libraries cannot have an indexed set of transparencies or slides providing samples from a wide range of index and abstract entries, catalog entries, and covers, title pages, and tables of contents or key resource tools. These aids could be used by librarians in the classroom or in the library. Certainly some pull-down screens could be installed in the library wherever classes are regularly held. Overhead projectors on portable carts can be available nearby, so that even impromptu classes can take advantage of the aids.

Whenever substantive AV aids are used, consideration should be given to providing them in handout form at the end of the learning period. If people know that the materials will be made available to them, they are free to relax and become involved with the presentation and discussion without needing to copy the material frantically into their notes. Waiting until the end of the session to give out the copies prevents the audience from reading ahead rather than participating.

Workbooks

Workbooks are among the more popular forms of library instruction. They make it possible to reach large numbers of people and allow the individual to work at his or her own pace. They can be used as assignments for groups of people or filled out independently by interested individuals. Some workbooks, aimed at users who are new to the library, are introductory tools that can equalize the level of library sophistication to provide a foundation for more advanced instructional efforts.[8] Others address different levels of need or focus on particular resources.[9]

The library at the University of California at Los Angeles pioneered the development of workbooks. Many libraries have adapted the UCLA model or have developed others, so that many examples are now available. A number of good articles on how workbooks should be constructed, implemented, and evaluated have been published.[10] One can even find practical advice on how to compile workbooks to prevent students from copying from each other or from all needing the same library materials at the same time.[11]

The worksheets or tests associated with workbooks can be self-graded, graded by a faculty member or librarian, or computer graded. If constructed well, the workbook and evaluation mechanisms need very little or no interpretation. Workbooks can also be used in conjunction with audiotapes or lectures. Consistent, extensive use of workbooks can provide ongoing data that help to document the scope of the program and the degree of student achievement in it.

Workbooks do take time to prepare and test, even though a wide variety of backup material is available. Yet workbooks prepared for commercial purposes, and there are an increasing number, may answer the needs of some libraries. Worksheets may provide more flexibility in timing and content for clients who are not totally unfamiliar with the library. At Brigham Young University, for example, students score their own pretests to determine which sections of the workbook they need to study and in what detail.[12] Workbooks are among the better developed and most widely used library instruction tools today, but there is still much room for improvement.

Programmed and Computer-assisted Instruction

Programmed instruction using books and computer-assisted instruction use the same learning theory. The theory is that the desired outcome of learning is to get students to make the proper responses to given stimuli. *Developing Programmed Instructional Materials* by James E. Espich and Bill Williams does an excellent job in outlining the planning that must go into developing programmed instructional materials and provides guidance in how to proceed. The basic approach that is suggested is:

1. To present the stimulus to the student
2. To help the student to make the desired response by giving clues, by leading toward it, or by giving the response itself
3. To reinforce immediately desired responses.[13]

Libraries have been slower to utilize these forms of instruction since they call for expertise that few librarians possess. But where such expertise is available or can be obtained from instructional support units, these opportunities should be explored, for they offer a means of reaching large numbers of learners with little or no investment of time, once preparation is completed. Both techniques also allow users maximum flexibility. Programmed instruction has a success rate comparable to that of other methods of instruction. Materials can be used for point-of-use instruction.[14] The advantage of printed programmed instruction over computer-assisted instruction (CAI) is cost. The latter is too expensive for some libraries; but where terminals are already available or can be afforded, it may well be worth the effort to seek out programming expertise. CAI has been successfully used at a number of institutions (e.g., Denver University[15] and

University of Illinois at Champaign-Urbana). Librarians interested in CAI are advised to see some existing programs in action. The technology for CAI is clearly available; the challenge is to produce high-quality programming.

Term-paper Clinics

Term-paper clinics are another popular form of library instruction. They are usually given in a lecture or workshop format. Their chief strength derives from the fact that students have an immediate need when they come to the clinic and thus are highly motivated. While some clinics will provide instruction to entire classes upon request and tailor the presentations to the general subject area of the assigned paper, most service is provided to people who sign up independently. For this reason, publicity is a key ingredient in busy and successful clinics. Publicity should include encouraging referrals from faculty as well as direct advertisement to potential clients. Publicity should clearly note the level of help available, i.e., whether the services are geared to the basic research level or to graduate students. Obviously, if a clinic seeks to meet the needs of all levels, some attempt needs must be made to group students of fairly equivalent abilities or needs together.

Scheduling term-paper clinics is also a serious problem. There is no perfect solution, and each library must make its own best guess, after consulting with faculty, and then continue to experiment year by year until there is evidence that the schedule is reasonably responsive to students' needs.

Term-paper clinics sometimes also include one-on-one counseling. Librarians may help teach research techniques at communication skills centers. Obviously, such individual efforts are highly time-consuming, but if there is a strong institutional commitment to student retention such instruction may be appropriate.

A Combination of Approaches

It is worth reiterating that there is no one ideal method of library instruction. Indeed, in tests comparing different methodologies for groups of learners, student performance has been as good following one type of instruction as another. One can say, however, that selectively combining different methodologies can strengthen the learning/teaching process.

9. Contents Selection and Timing

After the instructional objective and methodology for a particular learning experience have been determined, the next step is to consider systematically what the contents should be. As has already been underscored, at this point a great many librarians err by including too many items because they are "good" or "important" for the student to know, even though they may not directly relate to or support the achievement of the learning objective. Ruthlessness is called for at this point. If the learning objective can be achieved without inclusion of a particular piece of information or activity, that element should be omitted.

To provide further guidance in selecting contents, two philosophical questions should be addressed and agreed upon by those involved in the program. The first concerns the relationship of library instruction to the learners' other studies. The underlying philosophy might demand either that a particular target group be exposed to a complete coverage of appropriate library materials and skills or that only the learner's immediate needs be addressed. While most librarians would, at least theoretically, agree that not all students need exposure to atlases, special collections, or other materials clearly outside the realm of their interest, librarians tend to suffer from an overriding sense of guilt if they do not expose students to as many materials as possible within an identified interest area. For example, should not students in a basic course required for education majors be introduced to the card catalog, *The Education Index*, ERIC, juvenile encyclopedias, the curriculum library, government publications in the field of education, the collection of tests, and materials in appropriate sections of the reference collection and pamphlet file? Clearly the inclusion of all these items in a typical one-hour workshop is out of the question if the learning experience is to be a positive one.

If the students can be present on a series of occasions, the material may be presented in well-regulated "doses." Such a plan will raise the motivational level and allow for complete coverage of contents within a realistic period of time.

If, however, there is no assurance that the students will return to the library as a group, they can still be alerted to the literature of a field and its key access tools without sacrificing the quality of the primary learning experience. Two basic ways of approaching this need are to provide students with the appropriate learning matrix developed during the planning process (*see* Chapter 4, especially Figure 9) or with a pathfinder that includes a listing of important materials, subject headings, etc. A good example of a combined approach is shown in Figure 11, which is taken from a colorful guide to beginning research in history and social studies prepared for the secondary school level.[1] The guide is divided into five sections: The Most Recent Years, World Events, The United States, Places, and the section that is shown here, People. Across the page from a simplified flow chart is a listing of all titles shown. Each title is given a short descriptive entry, including how the material is arranged. Such a guide allows the learning experience to focus on the students' immediate needs, while at the same time it shows students where their current research efforts are located within the total resources of the field. A flow chart at the beginning of a workbook can provide an over-all subject resource orientation while still enabling students to pursue the specific problem on which they are working. When the emphasis is on meeting students' needs, rather than on a well-balanced, comprehensive user-education program, providing students with the *framework* within which their current needs are being met is a corollary responsibility.

The second philosophical decision that should be made is whether the library user-education program should be confined to the sponsoring library or expanded to include the resources of the community or region. School programs that include trips to nearby public or academic libraries, for example, push back the boundaries and expose learners to wider possibilities. To date, however, the trend has been to limit the programs to the resources at hand. Since, clearly, there is not enough time even to cover all of the resources within a given institution, confining the program seems to be a reasonable approach. However, from the learner's standpoint, mention should be made of the information resources of the wider community.

The combined effect of the continuing exponential growth of world publishing and the growing limitations on acquisition budgets means that a smaller and smaller proportion of the total output will be within the immediate reach of any library's users. Search strategies will increasingly, therefore, have to consider the resources of other libraries and agencies. Library instruction that includes information about accessing information from a variety of sources will be helpful throughout the user's life.

There should also be an effort to move away from emphasis on particular tools or resources to a greater concentration on concepts and research strategies. Increasing importance should be paid in school and academic libraries to ensuring that students have positive learning and working experiences with librarians rather than focusing on a particular set of library skills. This is important because once students complete their formal education they are much more likely to have the opportunity to turn for assistance to a librarian than to an instructor. Moreover, it is unlikely that any particular library tool will be remembered, or indeed will be applicable to later needs. What will be important will be the fact that the user has acquired the library habit and thinks of the librarian as a positive source of help when he or she has an information need.

Key Content Areas

When considering what should be included in the user-education program, six basic areas should be considered: attitudinal concerns, the logistics of using the library, the logistics of using resource tools, the organization of information, resources, and search strategies. In addition, some students may need survival skills. Though all of these areas have already been covered, a few points should be emphasized.

Detailed information on how to use the library effectively is essential: the hours the library is open, how to put a hold on a book, how the books are arranged. Such information is best given when it is needed, usually by way of handouts. It is important that attitudinal concerns be thought of and planned for in every activity of the user-education program. Fostering a positive learning experience should always be the goal.

The paramount role that search strategies should play in learning experiences has often been noted. Two hallmarks of good library instruction are: to start with the learners and their needs and to provide a real-life learning situation. If the introductory learning experience is a broad-based one, the instruction should emphasize the way in which a person would approach the library for specific information. If the learning experience is focused on a particular reference material, say, a periodical index, the instruction should emphasize the way in which an individual would approach the library for

BIOGRAPHY INDEX
    An index, like the Readers' Guide, to biographical material in both books and magazines.
    10 volumes, 1946 -- present.   Arranged in alphabetical order by last name of the person written about.

CHAMBERS' BIOGRAPHICAL DICTIONARY
    Includes "the great of all nations and all times." Has some 15,000 brief entries.
    1 volume.   Arranged in alphabetical order by last name.

CONCISE DICTIONARY OF AMERICAN BIOGRAPHY
    A condensed Dictionary of American Biography. Same number of biographies but shorter entries. See D.A.B. for full description.
    1 volume.   Arranged alphabetically by last name.

CONCISE DICTIONARY OF NATIONAL BIOGRAPHY
    A condensed Dictionary of National Biography. Same number of biographies but shorter entries. See D.N.B. for full description.
    2 volumes: Part I, to 1900; Part II, 1900 to 1950.   Each volume arranged alphabetically by last name.

CURRENT BIOGRAPHY
    Tries to cover all important contemporary people in all fields (musicians, statesmen, writers, magicians, etc.). Includes a photograph of the person. Some of the earlier books contain people who are now deceased; all entries were alive in the year of publication.
    38 volumes.   One index covers 1940-1970. The index of the latest 1970 volume (e.g., 1978 or 1979) indexes all of the 1970's.

DICTIONARY OF AMERICAN BIOGRAPHY
    Most comprehensive collection of short biographies of anyone who has become even well-known in some field. (Gamblers, botanists, doctors, swindlers, presidents, etc.) Covers people 1776-1940, with 5 supplements to 1955. Must be dead to be in the D.A.B..
    10 volumes, plus 5 volumes of supplements.   Arranged alphabetically by last name.

DICTIONARY OF NATIONAL BIOGRAPHY
    Comprehensive collection of short biographies of people of Great Britain from earliest historical period to present.
    22 volumes.   Arranged alphabetically by last name.

INTERNATIONAL WHO'S WHO
    Short biographies of well-known living people from almost any country in the world from all fields. Most information gathered from questionnaires, so it's not very objective.
    1 volume.   Arranged alphabetically by last name.

Figure 11.   Example of a combined pathfinder and matrix of learning needs. Reprinted from *Footprints: A Guide to Beginning Research in History and Social Studies* by Robert Skapura. Copyright © 1979 Robert Skapura. Reprinted by permission of the author.

MCGRAW-HILL ENCYCLOPEDIA OF WORLD BIOGRAPHY
Articles of fair length of people both living and dead. Includes not only
biographical information but also comments on their importance in history.
Usually contains a picture.
12 volumes.   Arranged alphabetically by last name.   Also an index in the
last volume.

READERS' GUIDE TO PERIODICAL LITERATURE
Index to well over 130 of the most popular magazines. Appears cluttered with
everything jammed together, but it remains the only index to so many popular
magazines. Most difficult task is to figure out what topic to look under. Only
practice makes this easier.
1 volume for each year.   Arranged in alphabetical order by subject and author.

THE STORY OF CIVILIZATION
Written by Will Durant, it is one of the most enjoyable history books to read.
All aspects covered: people, events, politics, culture, etc..
10 volumes, each volume covers one time period.   Index in each volume.

WEBSTER'S BIOGRAPHICAL DICTIONARY
Lists names of 40,000 noteworthy people both living and dead. Contains tables
of heads of state and high officials of various countries. Entries are rather
brief.
1 volume.   Arranged alphabetically by last name.

WHO WAS WHO IN AMERICA
Those who made it in Who's Who In America and then died are entered in Who Was
Who. See Who's Who for full description.
5 volumes from 1942-1970. Historical volume 1607-1896.   Arranged
alphabetically by last name.

WHO'S WHO
Persons of distinction in all fields in all parts of the world. Straight facts
on education and accomplishments. Not very descriptive.
1 volume.   Arranged alphabetically by last name.

WHO'S WHO IN AMERICA
Very brief description of living Americans of distinction in some field.
Information comes from questionnaires sent to the persons themselves, so it's
not very objective or descriptive. Good for a start if you have no idea what made
your person famous.
2 volumes.   Arranged alphabetically by last name.

WHO'S WHO IN THE WORLD
Very brief descriptions of living people with a worldwide reputation in some
field. Information comes from questionnaires sent to the persons themselves, so
it's not very descriptive. Good book to start with if you have no idea what makes
your person famous.
1 volume.   Arranged alphabetically by last name.

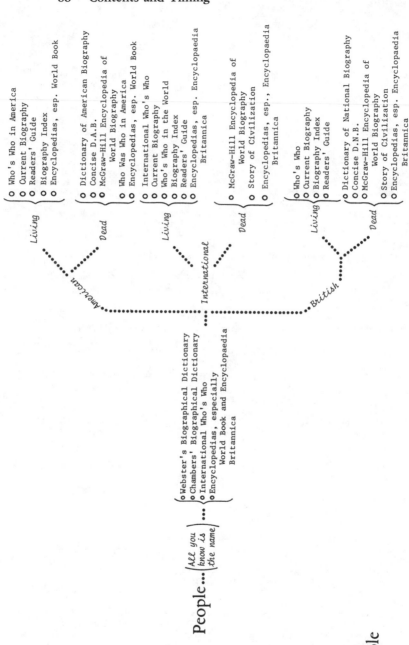

People

People...
$\left\{\begin{array}{l}\text{\textit{All you}}\\\text{\textit{know is}}\\\text{\textit{the name}}\end{array}\right\}$...
○ Webster's Biographical Dictionary
○ Chambers' Biographical Dictionary
○ International Who's Who
○ Encyclopedias, especially
   World Book and Encyclopaedia
   Britannica

American

Living
○ Who's Who in America
○ Current Biography
○ Readers' Guide
○ Biography Index
○ Encyclopedias, esp. World Book

Dead
○ Dictionary of American Biography
○ Concise D.A.B.
○ McGraw-Hill Encyclopedia of
   World Biography
○ Who Was Who in America
○ Encyclopedias, esp. World Book

International

Living
○ International Who's Who
○ Current Biography
○ Who's Who in the World
○ Biography Index
○ Readers' Guide
○ Encyclopedias, esp. Encyclopaedia
   Britannica

Dead
○ McGraw-Hill Encyclopedia of
   World Biography
○ Story of Civilization
○ Encyclopedias, esp., Encyclopaedia
   Britannica

British

Living
○ Who's Who
○ Current Biography
○ Biography Index
○ Readers' Guide

Dead
○ Dictionary of National Biography
○ Concise D.N.B.
○ McGraw-Hill Encyclopedia of
   World Biography
○ Story of Civilization
○ Encyclopedias, esp. Encyclopaedia
   Britannica

Figure 11. (cont.)

specific information in a journal. Never should the design begin with the library or its resources; it should always begin with the potential learners and their informational needs.

Contents in a Cumulating Program

Curriculum planning that grows from an analysis of the needs of target groups will invariably lead to the development of a series of learning experiences that build on top of each other. There is widespread acceptance of this multilevel approach to curriculum designing for library instruction, but no agreement about how many levels are appropriate. On the academic level, for example, Hazel Mews in her book, *Reader Instruction in Colleges and Universities*, suggests three main phases plus the opportunity for special activities "designed to spread knowledge and love of books and better understanding of libraries."[1] The introductory presentation near the beginning of the freshman year should promote "the impression both that the library is an important part of the academic institution, and that the library staff will be willing and anxious to help the students." The second stage allows for a great deal of flexibility and focuses on smoothing the way for readers to find needed material. The third stage covers literature in specific subject areas in some depth and provides guidance for preparing a major research paper. Other practitioners, however, suggest at least two phases during the freshman year and call for a continuous four-year undergraduate instruction program.[2] Certainly library instruction at the K–12 level should also progress in a logical, step-by-step fashion, each phase building on the previous one. Eventually, what is done at the elementary and secondary levels should provide the basis for curriculum planning at the college level and for defining the public library's instructional role with regard to students. Public library efforts should thus interface with those of the schools. At the moment, however, there is no generally accepted curriculum design at any level, and each effort develops its own.

Where one learning experience is designed to build upon another, or where a number of sections of a particular learning experience are given by more than one instructor, it is very important to have clear guidelines about the contents to be covered and the structure or approach to be employed. Such guidelines, combined with uniform instructional aids or handouts, can provide reasonable assurance that the majority of the students will acquire a common body of knowledge and master a common set of skills. Without consistency within a designated learning experience, it is impossible to develop a meaningful curriculum. Moreover, agreement in advance about contents and structure can save much time and effort among the instructors, who will not have to develop objectives, select contents, develop materials, etc., on their own. Thus time and creativity can be conserved for curriculum planning in other areas and, of course, for collectively refining shared responsibilities. Such joint planning does not mean that everyone will say or do exactly the same thing. The personality of a library instructor, the style of the classroom instructor, and the learners themselves will affect the learning experience in spite of the presence of a core of common experiences.

Contents in a Survival Skills Program

Special consideration should be given to contents that focus on what are commonly referred to as survival skills. Sometimes it will be said that it is impossible for people to learn how to use a library if they cannot read. However, there is evidence (*see* Chapter 14) that positive exposure toward librarians, libraries, and books may in fact do more to promote literacy and lifelong reading than is imagined. Moreover, information-handling skills can be of great help to the slow reader. Take, for example, a poor reader at the secondary or college level who has to make a speech or write a paper. The first problem (and one that is frequently a very difficult one for the student to surmount) is choosing a topic. The problems in selecting topics are well known to reference librarians who get request after request on a limited number of issues, such as the right to life, child abuse, and solar energy. Moreover, once a topic is selected the student has the problem of locating reference materials. How much easier for the student to browse through current magazines in the library, find an interesting article, and begin writing with one source already in hand.

Helping students discover how to judge the immediate value of a book by looking at its date of publication and its table of contents, by seeing if there is an index, and by reading the blurb about the author can save them much time and frustration. So can teaching them to skim material effectively, and to use digests, synopses, and the pamphlet file. Librarians should not keep such opportunities hidden from students, thereby forcing them to read every word in their assignments; librarians should be guides to shortcuts which can help students succeed with as little effort as possible. Helping students to succeed, to have positive learning experiences, and to develop the habit of coming to the library when they have information needs is, in fact, addressing the basic need in education today—preparing people for lifelong learning. In the long run, the development of the library habit may do more to promote literacy and reading than any other educational activity.

Instruction in survival skills may include teaching students how to alphabetize or how to look up words in a dictionary when they cannot spell. All such learning should take place either within the presentation of a search strategy or in response to a specific need. With all students, but particularly nontraditional students, the importance of seeing the relevance of what they are learning to something important to them cannot be overestimated.

Finally, what has been said about terminology (*see* Chapter 6) should be repeated here. Unless it is necessary for a learning experience, avoid library jargon. One can well use tracings without knowing the official term for them, and "magazines" can well replace the terms "journals" and "periodicals"—unless, of course, part of the learning objective is to distinguish between publications of scholarly and popular presses. The contents of the learning experience should always be limited to the requirements at hand.

Timing

The relationship between contents and timing of presentation has already been referred to more than once in this book. The ideal is to provide what is needed at the exact time it is needed. Timing affects motivation. Students will retain very little of what they learn from one year to the next, but the amount can be increased when learning experiences directly address immediate needs. Moreover, retention will also improve if students put into practice what they have just learned, and it will further improve if positive reinforcement occurs. Giving instruction too late is as bad as giving it too early. Motivation will drop significantly if all or most of the research has been completed; moreover, faulty search techniques may have been developed. Whenever possible, then, the sequence of the learning experience should be:

LEARNING NEED → LEARNING EXPERIENCE DESIGNED TO MEET NEED → LEARNING PUT INTO PRACTICE → POSITIVE REINFORCEMENT

Most public library instruction efforts, however, cannot be built around satisfying immediate needs. (Exceptions will be advertised workshops on genealogical studies or other areas of high general interest.) To maximize retention where learning needs cannot be grouped, every effort should be made to provide self-paced, discrete learning packages that can be used as individual needs arise: AV point-of-use materials, pathfinders, worksheets, and programmed instruction on specific topics or search strategies may be appropriate.

Timing is also influenced by competing demands on the user's time and interests. Giving library tours during freshman orientation week is a classic example of poor timing, since during this period new students' concerns are focused on getting to know professors, making friends, and generally finding their way around campus. If, for some reason, such library tours are deemed necessary, learning objectives should be limited to developing positive feelings about the library and librarians.

Where campuses have special programs to introduce students to the campus before the academic year, thought can be given to including library instruction among the activities. This time is better than orientation week, because students have not begun class assignments and are not in the process of "settling in." One of the most intriguing efforts of this type was developed at the University of New Hampshire. Along with a handbook mailed to incoming freshmen to introduce them to campus services, a self-corrected library competency test was sent. A follow-up questionnaire showed that 78 percent of those who received the mailing read the library section in the handbook, nearly all of that group took the test, and many worked to improve their library skills before coming to college.[3] Obviously, the timing was excellent, since many students had the time between the end of high school and the beginning of college to work at improving skills in an area that was clearly important to college success and that was known to require attention.

The length of the instruction sessions should be dictated largely by the objective and the contents. Thought should also be given to the potential attention span of the learners. Habit has a lot to do with spans of concentration. Although television has conditioned most adults to half-hour segments, small children will have considerably shorter attention spans. High-school students are used to the 50-minute hour (though program planners should bear in mind that it is unwise to present important material near the end of a class period). There is also a relationship between the sophistication of the medium being used and the attention span of learners. A general rule of thumb is that the longer the presentation, the more sophisticated the medium should be. For example, an audiotape would not hold a learner's interest for a 30-minute presentation, but a film or videotape might be successful.

The alternative to shorter time frames is to break the session into smaller segments. Brief presentations, alternated with brief practice periods, are effective. Such a plan allows learners to put the information presented immediately into practice. If explanations in self-paced materials or work-sheets are too long, learners will tune out. Pretesting such presentations is the best way to assure that the length of the materials is both suitable and realistic.

The order of presentation is another important aspect of timing. Contents should be arranged in a logical fashion that approximates the way in which the *learner* would approach the problem or material in a real-life situation. Though an introductory overview, followed by the highlighting of a long series of particular resources, is frequently the librarian's natural approach, the learner is more likely to attack the material like a detective: there are one or two pieces of needed information out there someplace. How do I concentrate on finding just those items? Of course there are exceptions. A research team moving into a new project area will be more likely to use the approach that is characteristic of the librarian. But in this case, too, it is well to design the learning experience so that it will reflect the usual learner's approach and provide the group with a basic guide on how to begin future research efforts.

10. Evaluation

Probably more concern is expressed and less action taken about evaluation than any other aspect of library instruction. This is understandable from a number of perspectives. First, within librarianship there has been little evaluation of *any* reader service. Second, educational evaluation in general has not progressed beyond pencil-and-paper testing and the grading of occasional papers. Third, educators as a group have been reluctant to evaluate the over-all results of their endeavors, preferring to evaluate students after completion of each unit and assuming that the accumulation of a certain number of successfully completed units equals a high school education or is sufficient preparation for a certain level of competency within a particular discipline.

Beginning in the early sixties, however, it became increasingly clear that the public was tired of teachers who could not teach. While the disenchantment initially focused on inadequately prepared public school teachers, dissatisfaction with other academic areas soon surfaced as well. For the first time college students sued universities for failure to provide them with "promised" education. Much of the impetus for competency-based education grew out of this disenchantment.

Why is it that educators in general and librarians in particular are not enthusiastic about evaluating the outcomes of their efforts? The answer is threefold: shortage of time, lack of knowledge, and fear. The professor loaded down with 60 or 90 tests or papers to grade in the 48 hours before final grades are due at the registrar's office is not an uncommon picture. It is obvious that such pressured efforts at evaluation can be of only limited value. More enterprising or more fortunate professors may have graduate assistants or computers to help them or will move up the exam dates to allow for more time and possibly a review of the tests with the classes. In some cases grading may be less time-consuming than preparation of the tool of measurement. To develop a good multiple-choice answer test is an extremely difficult task, and to develop a true-and-false test is not easier. Whether the bulk of the time is spent at the beginning or at the end, evaluation is a time-consuming process.

Few instructors and even fewer librarians have had formal training in evaluation techniques. One tends, of course, to replicate the kind of evaluation with which one was evaluated. So despite the fact that there seems to be little correlation between students' abilities to pass spelling tests and their ability to spell correctly when writing a letter, week after week children's spelling is evaluated by having them spell words from designated lists. Matching the parts of a catalog card as shown in an illustration with a list of terms is similarly a futile way of learning to locate information. There is also a very real element of fear involved with any type of testing—not just on the part of the person taking the test but on the part of the instructor as well. This is particularly true if one is attempting to evaluate learner outcome, i.e., what the student has actually mastered. Take, for example, a class in "new math." When the mid-term exam is handed out, the students discover not only that they can not work out most of the problems but also most of the questions do not seem to bear any resemblance to any work covered to date. At the next class period, the teacher soundly berates the class because everyone did so poorly that the teacher had to add a set number of points to all of the grades so that at least some of them would pass. In such a case it is not the class that has failed; it is the teacher. Either the teaching/learning experience was faulty or the test did not evaluate what the students had been learning.

Evaluation must begin by asking fundamental questions: how willing are librarians to be held accountable and how committed are they to developing the best library user-education programs possible? It is easy to cloak fears in such grand sounding phrases as "We have so little time with the students that we don't want to waste it on testing them" or "Library tests will only turn the students off; I want them to like the library." The fact of the matter is that unless there is some kind of evaluation there is no way of knowing whether or not students are learning what was intended, whether they are being instructed in the most effective manner possible, what kind of attitudes the learners are forming about libraries, or what the educational value of library-related instruction is. Moreover, without evaluation it is impossible to improve the instructional program in any systematic manner.

In planning library instruction good evaluation is necessary on two levels: it provides the information necessary to improve individual teaching/learning efforts, and it provides information necessary for over-all program planning, i.e., for the effective deployment of limited human and financial resources so as to offer the best possible instructional program to as many students as possible. Evaluation takes some of the guesswork out of instruction and brings final results more within control. It pinpoints weaknesses that require supportive action. It gives confidence to those within the program and documentation to those outside. It helps people to discover the limitations of their knowledge and abilities and to take pride in their accomplishments.

Evaluation is never perfect. Evaluation is simply a means for improving decision-making. The extent to which the process is beneficial depends on the degree to which it offers answers to the questions being asked either inside or outside of the library. The value of the information produced can sometimes be improved by using several different evaluative procedures, but sufficient planning in advance of the actual evaluation is always crucial to its success.

The process of planning for evaluation parallels the planning process described in Chapter 3. It focuses on determining what questions need answering. Which are formative questions, i.e., which questions are designed to guide future developments? Which questions are summative, i.e., which are designed to provide final conclusions about the validity of an effort? For whom are the answers intended—librarians, faculty, administrators, students, a funding source? What questions have priority? What resources can be secured for doing the evaluations? What contents should be included? What method of evaluation is most appropriate?

Planning for evaluation before the instruction begins will help to ensure that the library will concentrate its efforts in the right areas. Some evaluation techniques, in fact, can be used only if they are begun before a new program is initiated. For example, if a library unit is to be required in a writing course, unless data (i.e., grades, papers written) are obtained for the year before the unit is offered, there will be no possibility of "before and after" comparisons on student performance.

No discussion of evaluation for library instruction programs should ignore the Model Statement of Objectives developed by the ACRL Bibliographic Instruction Section.[1] Yet it should be remembered that this is a model statement only, and that it consists of guidelines developed in a context totally removed from the particular needs of particular students. If this caveat is borne in mind, the guidelines can serve as one of a series of checks when reviewing an over-all program plan.

There are five distinct yet overlapping areas of concern in evaluating library instruction. They are:

> Evaluating learning outcomes
> Evaluating learning experiences
> Evaluating instructors
> Evaluating learners' attitudes
> Evaluating the over-all program.

The rest of this chapter will explore possible approaches to evaluation within these areas and the purposes for which each set of resultant data could be used. Detailed directions for how to develop individual tools are not included. Such information can be found in the literature of the social sciences or through consultants or units available on some campuses or in some school districts to help instructors develop evaluation tools and techniques. Tools developed by others are often available for adaptation. The Library Orientation-Instruction Exchange (LOEX), for example, has many library skills tests which can be borrowed upon request.

Evaluating Learning Outcomes

Evaluating learning outcomes has been covered to some extent in the chapter on setting objectives. Evaluating learning outcomes means determining whether or not the learning experience accomplished what it was designed to do; i.e., can the learners actually perform as stated in the objective? Good objectives will also specify the level at which the concept or skill can be considered to be mastered. For example, is it enough for a learner simply to find an article by using an index, should he or she be able to find an article of a certain type or date, or must it be suitable for a particular assignment? Such criteria can address levels of accuracy, speed, or quality, specifying when competence is sufficient to enable the learner to go on to the next step or to allow him or her to be considered to have successfully completed the learning experience.

Typical means of evaluating learning outcomes include the ability of students to obtain materials for class assignments and the quality of bibliographies,[2] over-all research papers, or oral reports. Some user-education programs have concentrated on the search process itself by having learners keep logs or journals outlining their research activities.[3] Such processes are time-consuming for both the learner and the evaluator, but they can provide for in-depth analysis of search procedures and indicate ways to improve an individual's skills. The greatest difficulty lies in convincing students of the value in participating in such a time-consuming effort. In the case of self-paced materials, including computer-assisted instruction, the evaluation is built naturally into the completion of the program, for it is impossible to complete the program unless the learner can give the right responses in structured situations.

Another whole level of evaluating learner outcomes addresses broader educational goals. How can one assess the relationship of library instruction to increased library use, to improved or increased reading, to better academic success, or to student retention? How successful is the user-education program in preparing people for lifelong learning, in helping them to function effectively in an information-rich but knowledge-poor society? Well-documented correlations in these areas will gain the interest not only of learners but also of the total academic community. Positive results can well lead to additional financial support, even in times of generally declining budgets, for any program that can be proven to promote literacy or academic success in a cost-effective manner is a highly salable one.

Several basic approaches seem promising for evaluating such learner outcomes. Controlled experiments employing before-and-after groups or control groups are one possibility. If enough conditions can be controlled, it should be possible to document the positive effect of library instruction on specific target groups. If an experimental group of high-risk students, for example, has a significantly higher retention rate than a control group, a case can be made for the value of the library instruction and the advantage of funding it for all high-risk students.

A second approach is to do longitudinal studies of comparable groups of students or matched pairs of students throughout their academic careers, comparing the academic success of those who participated in the user-education programs with those in the control group. Moreover, if the program has been in existence for a number of years and if there is clear documentation about which graduates participated in it, comparable groups or matched pairs of alumni might be compared to determine the effect of the user-education program on career advancement, future use of libraries, later independent study, amount of reading, and likelihood of graduate or postgraduate education. Studies undertaken by means of alumni questionnaires or in-depth interviewing can be of interest even though no evaluation may have been made during the time of library instruction.

Such evaluations require access to student records and the ability to track students over long periods of time. In most cases they will require support from research personnel, who can make sure that they are on a statistically sound footing and that the measurement tools are valid (for example, that the sample groups are large enough and that a sufficient number of pairs are matched).

In library literature there are examples of evaluations that may be used as springboards to more ambitious and sounder efforts. At a community college in the 1930s it was documented that

> during the period that the faculty has stressed the effective use of the library in teaching, the circulation of books has greatly increased. In the five years immediately preceding college-wide emphasis upon library instructional relationships the average student annually borrowed nine books, excluding books on reserve shelves, from the College library. During the past five years the average student has borrowed more than thirty books—more than three times the previous figure. [4]

One study found a correlation between grade-point average and use of the college library. [5] A significant correlation between library use and retention among college freshmen in certain subjects was found at another institution. [6] In experiments with institutionalized youths, concentrated exposure to books was found to have a positive effect on their future success. [7] Advances in automation have made it possible to keep a record on circulation and library usage. What is surprising is that to date so little in-depth research of this nature has been conducted.

Evaluations of this type require long-term commitment of resources. They are, however, directed at the heart of what most librarians involved in library instruction intuitively feel are the long-term outcome of their efforts. Moreover, such evaluations address central concerns of education today. If such efforts are too large for individual libraries, cooperative efforts or outside funding may afford solutions. If user-education programs cannot document their contributions to such learner outcomes, revisions of program goals and improvement of programs may be required. Where user-education programs can document significant contributions, their futures are assured.

Evaluating the Learning Experience

Evaluation of college-level courses, usually by the student government, represents an attempt to provide guidance for students in planning their academic programs. Evaluation of the teachers is usually included; it is also helpful to those who wish to improve their teaching and who wish support for applications for promotion or tenure.

The library instruction program can benefit from evaluation both immediately after an instruction session and at the end of the course in which the instruction was offered. Student response immediately after a presentation will often differ from an evaluation administered after there has been time to put learning into practice; on the other hand, by then details of the learning experience will have faded. Therefore, the initial student questionnaire can be particularly useful in determining how interesting and well organized the learning experience was and how appropriate the level of the material and discussion were to student needs. It can also lead to concrete suggestions about how the different aspects of the presentation could be improved. Follow-up questionnaires will elicit more accurate responses about how useful the learning experience was, how appropriate the timing was, and in what ways contents should be expanded or eliminated.

Because of the relative shortness of most library instruction presentations, the evaluative procedures should be brief. The questions included should be carefully chosen to match learning objectives and to derive information from which strengths and weaknesses in the learning experience can be identified. The questionnaires in Figures 12 and 13 would be appropriate for evaluating a course-related library workshop in introductory level courses immediately after the presentation and at the end of the semester.

Follow-up questions about the library instruction unit can also be included in an over-all course evaluation rather than in a separate questionnaire. Such an approach reinforces the feeling that library instruction is an integral part of the course. There are other advantages to such an inclusion as well. At the end of a management course for which an evaluation questionnaire was administered, students unanimously cited the library unit on funding sources as the most valuable learning experience—and an unexpected one. When a library questionnaire is included as part of a general course evaluation, however, care should be taken to make sure that the results are made available and that they do not get "buried" in a mass of other data. It is also a good practice to have either the classroom instructor or a student administer the questionnaires, depending on campus practice. Doing so adds an air of objectivity to the proceedings that is absent if the librarian is present. In turn, if the questionnaire is completely controlled by the library, care should be taken to discuss the summarized results with the classroom instructor, in order to consider how the library component of the course can be improved.

Similar questionnaires can be used with "volunteer classes," like those at public libraries, and with independent learning experiences like pathfinders or point-of-use materials. Again the emphasis should be on brevity

---

Class: _____   Date: _____
Section: _____

1. The library presentation was

   |——————————|——————————|——————————|——————————|

   very well   well   somewhat   poorly   very poorly
   organized   organized   organized   organized   organized

2. The library presentation was

   |——————————|——————————|——————————|——————————|

   very   somewhat   not very   not at all
   interesting   interesting   interesting   interesting   interesting

3. Of the material presented, I knew

   |——————————|——————————|——————————|——————————|

   all of it   most of it   some of it   little of it   none of it

4. In terms of my work for this course, I think the information covered will be

   |——————————|——————————|——————————|——————————|

   very   moderately   of little   of no
   valuable   valuable   valuable   value   value

5. I wish the presentation had included: _____

   _____

   _____

Figure 12.   Evaluation for general course-related library workshop

and on eliciting data that can be used for the improvement of future learning experiences. Figure 14 shows an example of an evaluation which could be put at the end of a pathfinder. Obviously, not every person who independently uses such materials will complete the questionnaire, but those who feel strongly "for" or "against" are likely to respond if responding does not take too much time and if it is clear that there will be some follow-through. Librarians who regularly speak encouraging words while guiding patrons to pathfinders, noting how evaluations help to improve the program, can do much to increase the number of those who are willing to take the time to answer.

It is advisable to try out all learning experiences before formally offering them. Librarians who will be conducting a workshop for the first time should have the opportunity to practice on some group (e.g., student

Class: _____   Date: _____
Section: _____

1. In terms of the work I did for this course, the library presentation was

| |————————————|————————————|————————————| |

very   valuable   moderately   of little   of no
valuable   valuable   value   value

2. In terms of my other courses, the library presentation was

| |————————————|————————————|————————————| |

very   valuable   moderately   of little   of no
valuable   valuable   value   value

3. This semester I have used the library
   _____ 0 times
   _____ 1 time
   _____ 2–5 times
   _____ 6–9 times
   _____ 10 or more times

Figure 13.   End-of-semester evaluation for general library workshop

employees of the library) in a supportive climate in which the audience freely interacts with the new instructor. All self-paced learning materials and AV presentations should be pilot-tested in such a way and refined before being presented to learners. Far too often the material covered, the amount covered, or the style of the presentation is inappropriate for the target audience; there is simply no way to be sure without testing in advance. Humor, in particular, is very difficult for most amateurs to put across and should have wide testing before becoming part of a public presentation. Moreover, recurrent testing is needed to ensure that materials have not been outdated and that the style is still appropriate for current target groups. The results of such evaluations can be integrated into some formats more easily than others. Workshops can almost immediately be adjusted, but a videotape is obviously very difficult to update.

The pre- and post-tests for library skills are familiar means of evaluating the results of library instruction. Such tests, however, are difficult to construct, and interpreting their results can also present problems.[8] The more valuable of the two is the pre-test. If it is well constructed, and especially if it is clearly geared to the interests of the learners, the process can serve as a learning device in its own right, for it helps learners to comprehend the scope of information that is available to them as well as to

---

(NAME OF PUBLICATION)

Please take a moment to complete the following questionnaire and return it to any library employee. Your responses will be studied to help guide future library publications.

Thanks.

I used this publication for:
☐ Class Assignment   ☐ Term Paper
☐ Personal Research   ☐ Other

I found it:
☐ Very Useful   ☐ Useful   ☐ Not Useful

I liked the following *BEST* about this publication:

_____

_____

I liked the following *LEAST* about this publication:

_____

_____

Suggestions for improving the publication (e.g., additions to the guide, deletions, organization of the guide, etc.):

_____

_____

Status:
☐ Faculty   ☐ Staff
☐ Grad Student   ☐ Undergrad Student
                    ☐ Other

Figure 14.   User evaluation for pathfinder

recognize their own lack of knowledge. If administered long enough in advance, pretests can also be used for diagnostic purposes, and the instruction can be tailored to the specific needs of the target group. Pretesting should also serve as a means of exempting students who demonstrate proficiency in the areas to be covered. In schools that do diagnostic testing for English and math placement of incoming students, some thought should be given to promoting a library/research skills test to be administered at the same time. To frame a successful placement test requires a clear notion of the levels of performance that will be judged adequate and of the remedial learning opportunities that will be provided or required for students who fall below that level. Pretesting is also valuable in documenting learning needs. Too many faculty and administrators erroneously believe that their students know how to use the library, and test scores can dispel this notion much more quickly than sermons by librarians.

Post-tests are of less value. They can, however, document improvement in library skills and increased familiarity with library resources. They can therefore be useful political tools in making a case for the value of library instruction.

Completed post-tests should be carefully reviewed to determine where instruction has failed or where a question requires revision. Whenever possible, post-tests should be reviewed with learners, too, to show them what they missed and the areas that they still need to study. Ideally, the post-test can serve as a second diagnostic test, oriented toward the individual. Standardized tests in library skills administered during elementary and secondary years can motivate administrative and teacher concern for library instruction.

Having another instructor sit in on a presentation and critique the learning experience is also helpful. This evaluation should include all aspects of the program—instructional aids and the materials handed out, the assignments given, the amount of material covered, the quality of the discussion, and the organization of the presentation. Comments should also be made on the personal qualities of the instructor—how well he or she interacted with the class, his or her ability to hold students' interest, and clarity of expression. Such input should not be requested, however, unless it is really desired; the best way to show appreciation to those who take the time to make suggestions is to make appropriate improvements in the learning experience. The critic could be another librarian, an instructional development expert, or the classroom instructor who requested the library presentation. In the latter case it is important to let the instructor know that comments and suggestions are seriously wanted, and care must be taken not to become defensive when they are offered. Sometimes the most valuable criticisms are, in fact, unintended. One librarian, who for years had prided herself on the quality of her basic library workshop for freshman English courses, suddenly realized that awed instructors' comments that they were unfamiliar with a good deal of the material covered in her 50-minute presentation indicated either that the level of the presentation or the amount of material covered was too ambitious.

Videotaping instructional sessions allows instructors to see themselves as others do. Just this process may foster improved presentations. However, discussion of the presentation with peers can prove particularly rewarding.

Again it is important that the climate be supportive rather than judgmental. If, for example, parts of tapes of a number of different people are reviewed in one session, the experience should prove to be positive for everyone. Such sessions should emphasize situations that are particularly well handled and point up common problems. People who have serious difficulties giving effective presentations should review their own tapes with just their supervisor or the head of library instruction. Such discussion should lead to a detailed plan for improvement and a date for a follow-up evaluation. Plans might include working with a more experienced librarian, developing instructional aids and taking a course in teaching techniques.

Evaluating Instructors

It has already been pointed out that student comments on courses or workshops, criticism by a peer attending a session, and review of the videotape of a session are productive methods of evaluation. The librarian's success as an instructor can also be measured by an increase over time in the number of requests for his or her presentation. The gradual acceptance of a particular librarian as a teaching partner in the classroom is another welcome sign of a positive judgment.

No area of evaluation is more fraught with fear than that of evaluating librarians as instructors. Initially such evaluations should be only informative. Librarians who have not been trained as teachers are especially in need of support. Evaluations that can help them identify weaknesses and strengths should be seen as part of that effort. Administrative and peer encouragement to participate in workshops and courses and to work with others in a learning environment is essential if the instructor is to make improvement in the areas identified. In a new program it is important to bring instructional efforts up to an acceptable, if not a high, level as quickly as possible; the library user-education program cannot prosper otherwise. If librarians avoid evaluation because they fear negative judgments, improvement of the instruction program will be deterred. Far better to declare a learning period for everyone involved and guarantee that, for the duration of that period, no one's personnel record will be affected by his or her instructional evaluation. Of course, if after a reasonable length of time, library instruction is to remain a part of the librarian's responsibilities, it will quite properly be considered in evaluating new and current personnel. It is to be hoped that those librarians who, for whatever reason, cannot perform well in a direct teaching role, can find alternative ways to participate in user-education programs by developing pathfinders, point-of-use materials, and evaluation questionnaires.

Evaluating Learners' Attitudes

There are two basic means of evaluating learners' attitudes toward libraries and librarians. One is simply to ask them for their reactions. The other is to measure their use of the library. The brief questionnaire shown in Figure 15 shows how students' attitudes could be queried in a few moments. Administering such questionnaires both before and somewhat after library instruction will help to determine whether it has affected students' attitudes. Obviously, the tool section of the questionnaire can be more narrowly focused.

Many libraries have administered much more extensive questionnaires to determine user satisfaction with library services and resources. These are difficult tools to develop, and appropriate sampling is important if the resulting data are to be reliable. Thought must be given, for example, to whether the questionnaire is to be administered to library users only or to nonusers as well. If a neutral party analyzes the data, nonlibrary personnel will be more apt to accept the results as valid. Although public libraries more than others have used this type of evaluation, examples of questionnaires applicable to all types of libraries are available. Whenever such an

---

Name: | Sex: M   F | 1st semester: yes   no

A. HOW WOULD YOU GRADE THE LIBRARY SERVICES/FACILITIES YOU HAVE USED?
Do so by marking (+) *good,*   (OK) *satisfactory,*   (−) *poor,*   ( ) *have not used*:

( ) place to study	( ) journals	( ) reference books
( ) reserve reading	( ) interlibrary loan	( ) reference questions
( ) general reading	( ) microforms	( ) browsing
( ) borrowing books	( ) maps	( ) card catalog
( ) xerox service	( ) indexes, abstracts	( ) research

B. YOUR PATTERN OF LIBRARY USE?
Mark with (X):
( ) more than once a week
( ) more than 8 times a semester
( ) a few times
( ) none

C. DID YOU ASK FOR HELP FROM ANY LIBRARY WORKER?   Mark with (X):
( ) yes   ( ) no
WERE YOU SATISFIED?
( ) yes   ( ) no

Figure 15.   Student questionnaire on use of the library and library tools

ambitious undertaking is being considered, care should be taken to understand clearly why the questionnaire is being administered as well as to agree that changes will be effected as a result of findings. Why, for example, ask about the need for extended hours if there is no intention to change them? A variation on the written questionnaire would be the personal interview.

The other way of measuring attitudes is to measure changes in library use. The ultimate test, after all, is not what people say about how they feel about the library but whether or not they use it. Students and faculties can be queried regarding their use of the library, and additional data may become easily accessible with the introduction of automated circulation systems. Although records of checkouts by individuals cannot generally be monitored, computer statistics on subject areas are usually available. Thus, if a new instruction program is being initiated, significant increases in checkout of materials in the relevant subject area would be one indication of increased library use due to the instruction. In smaller institutions, the librarian may get an answer simply by recognizing students from workshops. Increased demand for instruction is another concrete indication of positive attitudes on the part of clientele.

Evaluating the Over-all Program

Once a year all evaluation data should be analyzed and an annual report prepared on the successes and failures of the user-education program. First, the program objectives that were set should be evaluated. Statistics on the number of faculty contacts, workshops given, and instructional materials produced should be compared with similar data from earlier years. Political accomplishments—e.g., courses now requiring a library component—should be documented. Summaries of the evaluation of particular learning experiences should also be prepared.

Evaluations of a "softer" nature may be included. Have letters of appreciation for an instruction activity been received from participants? Have comments been made in a suggestion box or book? Excerpts from such materials cannot take the place of more systematic evaluations, but they can certainly complement other documentation and add interesting examples to the annual report. Copies of all written comments should be kept (this may take some effort, since frequently the letters of appreciation will go to the librarian who was responsible for the activity). Interaction with library advisory or Friends' groups can also provide opportunities for ongoing evaluation, as can meetings especially called for candid discussion of the program.

Once the program is well under way, consideration should be given to having an outside consultant come in as an evaluator. The accumulation of data over several years will facilitate the process. The value to be derived from having a knowledgeable outsider take a fresh look at the user-education program can be considerable, particularly if the subsequent report can be used effectively with the library and institutional administrations.

The cost effectiveness of the program must be included in its over-all evaluation. Libraries are labor-intensive operations, and library instruction is no exception. Appropriate questions should be regularly asked; e.g., is the program providing an acceptable return for the investment of staff time being made? Are there more cost-effective approaches for any of the various efforts under way? Only if such questions are honestly asked and honestly answered can continued positive growth be assured for the program in the years to come.

In the school or academic library, the instruction program can be considered successful when curriculum discussions in subject areas regularly include librarians, and when the learning/teaching process reflects a sophisticated and extensive utilization of library resources. The purpose of all evaluation is to ensure cost-effective progress toward these goals.

11. Staffing Resources

Patterns of staffing in libraries are changing in a variety of ways. The causes for such changes range from the automation of library operations to the growing trend in which nonlibrary-trained administrators are hired for specialized functions such as personnel management and development. The library user-education program will necessitate further changes in staffing patterns. The initiation or expansion of this service will require librarians to spend more time working with faculty in such areas as planning, collection development, and instruction.[1] Within the existing resources of any particular library situation, a variety of staffing patterns may be possible and should be explored.

Since it goes without saying that most librarians have had no formal training in teaching, audiovisual production, or curriculum development, staff development programs will be the first priority as a library becomes deeply involved in instruction activities. Faculty from a school of education or communications department, or staff from instructional development or evaluation units might be tapped for some in-house instruction for all librarians; local librarians with particular expertise might be invited in to offer a lecture or workshop. Too often conference meetings and programs, including those held annually at Eastern Michigan University, and the workshops sponsored by library schools, ALA, or regional and state associations are pitched at the lowest common denominator. While librarians just becoming active in user-education programs have obvious needs, it is harder to find programs that address the needs of the more experienced instruction librarian. One example of an in-depth learning experience has been the 30-hour, one-week seminars held at the Columbia School of Library Services, which have been geared to practicing academic librarians with extensive involvement in library instruction. Attendance at such an in-depth program offers a unique opportunity to librarians who can then conduct in-house workshops upon return to their own communities.

To be successful, the staffing pattern for a comprehensive program of library instruction must involve cooperation between librarians and classroom teachers. Cooperation is especially critical at the beginning, at the planning stage. This is a time for mutual education, and without a careful melding of learning objectives at this point, it is unlikely that noteworthy progress will be made. At this stage the librarian learns in detail what it is that the instructors are hoping to accomplish in their classes, and the instructors learn how library skills and resources can help them meet their objectives. Teachers may consequently incorporate the library component into their assignments or course outlines at the most appropriate time or may decide that their students require more background work in general library skills before learning about specialized resources.

This cooperation between librarians and teachers may extend to the joint development of self-paced materials or instructional aids. On the other hand, it may seem more productive for the classroom instructor to critique materials developed by the librarian. Where large numbers of students are involved, cooperative efforts will eventually focus on developing materials, though perhaps it is best to delay doing so until the relationship between instructors and librarians has developed to the point that there is a shared vision of desired outcomes and a good climate of give-and-take.

An agreement should be reached between librarians and teachers about how the library instruction component will be evaluated, and how the evaluation may serve as the basis for developing a library instruction program for the following semester or year.

Discussion is certainly appropriate at this point as to who will be responsible for what aspects of the library-based learning experience. Would the faculty member like to do the teaching? If so, how can the librarian assist? Instructional aids can provide classroom faculty with good examples of all the agreed-upon materials, helping to ensure that nothing is overlooked and alerting faculty members in advance of the instruction they will give. If the librarian is to do the teaching, how can faculty members develop student interest? The better the initial planning, in fact, the less it matters who does the actual teaching.

In school and academic settings, suggestions that all library instruction should be done by the classroom instructors or, on the other hand, by librarians are pointless, since neither alternative is realistic. To expect faculty to keep up with all the latest resource materials, on-line data bases, etc., and to be comfortable with the basic research strategies and reference materials to which students at beginning levels need exposure is as unrealistic as expecting that librarians can—given typical student-librarian ratios—maintain all necessary library operations and offer a comprehensive user-education program as well.

In large universities, graduate assistants and teaching assistants are often the most likely candidates to supplement the teaching capabilities of the librarians. But here there is a twofold motivation problem: getting the departmental faculty to motivate the teaching assistants to motivate the students. Librarians may have an opportunity to inspire the teaching assistants during a training period, but since the teaching assistants are in no way accountable to the library, it is highly desirable to have some reinforcement from the faculty or the department head. If there are large numbers of students, working through teaching assistants may be the only way to provide library units in required courses.

The situation for public libraries is usually quite different. Teamwork occurs only when instructional activities are planned in conjunction with local schoolteachers. For the most part, responsibilities for determining learning objectives for specified groups and for implementing the learning experiences rest with library personnel. The public library user-education program, to a much greater degree than in school and academic library settings, succeeds or fails on the skills and competence of the librarians.

There are ways of enhancing the teaching capabilities of all types of libraries. Since, for example, a number of libraries already work with teaching assistants or similar groups (e.g., skills centers tutors), it seems logical to consider nonprofessional library staff as contributors to the instruction program. Of course, utilizing these nonprofessionals will be totally out of the question if the real reason why librarians have such programs is, as Pauline Wilson[2] and others suggest, to enchance their own image as librarians or (in academic institutions) to support their claims to faculty status. If, however, the goal of the library is to provide the best instruction program possible within the framework of the institution's priorities and limited resources, then the possibility of using library support staff in some aspects of the instruction program should be explored. Just as teaching assistants are used to teach basic courses, grade papers, and do background research work, support staff or graduate assistants may fill similar roles in the library instruction program. Many libraries have paraprofessionals who hold doctoral degrees in subject areas. Their expertise can enrich user-education programs, provided that they are interested and that sufficient funds exist to compensate them. Enthusiastic support staff are infinitely preferable to reluctant professionals pressed into service.

Using students to help in the instruction program is another option. Students who have recently mastered new knowledge or skills are often excellent teachers of their peers. Not only can students employed by the library help in a peer-tutoring function, but also students who already know the material being covered or who learn it quickly can sometimes be enlisted on an ad hoc basis. Individual attention can often make the difference in a slow learner's success.

Idealistic talk about involving all librarians in the library instruction program—happily few libraries are guilty of it!—can create a good deal of unnecessary anxiety among the staff. As has been discussed in Chapter 2, many librarians not only are not interested in teaching, but also are frightened at the prospect of doing so. Unleashing such fears may well create negative currents about the entire program. If staff members are forced to participate, either directly or indirectly through pressures for promotion or tenure, there will be little gained; such librarians usually make poor teachers. On the other hand, nothing should prevent the technical services librarian or bibliographer who wants to teach from doing so. The experience will widen his or her professional horizons and enrich the performance of that person's primary responsibilities. (It is worth noting that one of the first study groups in the American Library Association Library Instruction Round Table during 1978/79 dealt with the role of technical services librarians in library instruction.) Such participation will not only provide a richer human resource pool—something desperately needed early after the beginning of each academic session—but it will also frequently broaden the support for the program within the library itself and perhaps even break down traditional barriers between technical and public services librarians.

Volunteerism had a very bad name among libraries for many years, but as money tightened during the seventies, public libraries in particular took another look at this resource. The University of Colorado at Boulder, for example, has obtained volunteers through the University of Colorado Women's Club for years. These women are regularly recruited for such activities as working at the circulation desk and tattle-taping books. Volunteers can be used to advantage in the library instruction program, especially in the preparation of materials, but perhaps also in direct involvement with selected teaching/learning experiences. Can a volunteer be found who will work with library personnel in developing clear, attractive signs at the microfilm readers to save staff from having to give one-to-one instruction? Is there a volunteer experienced in public relations or publicity who can help with the preparation of library handouts? Can a faculty member's wife, possibly with an advanced degree, conduct some of the fall orientation tours or help correct questionnaires or tests? (Her involvement may also encourage her husband to become interested in the library instruction program.) Library school students may be particularly useful.

Volunteers can save time for library personnel. It may be that better directional signs are needed before work on another objective can begin; perhaps no staff time will be available unless the number of personnel needed to staff the reference desk is reduced. Freeing librarians from giving directions may allow them to develop a course outline or a self-paced workbook. As budgets remain unchanged or decrease in actual buying power, planning will involve such trade offs more and more, and libraries interested in developing instruction programs will be well advised to be as imaginative as possible in their attitudes toward staff utilization.

Another way to extend the staffing resources of the library instruction program is to beg, borrow, or steal materials others have prepared. The state and regional library instruction clearinghouses and LOEX offer a wide variety of instructional materials for loan at no cost other than postage. Information on nearby clearinghouses can usually be obtained by writing to the area ACRL office. The clearinghouses make no attempt to evaluate the materials sent to them, and so there is much dross. If, however, responses to an enquiry by the executive director of LOEX can be accepted as valid,[3] many useful sample materials are available. Wading through dozens of workbooks looking for good models and examples consumes less time than starting from scratch. Indeed, a basic principle of library instruction is not to reinvent the wheel!

Look beyond library sources. Much material in the social sciences applies to library instruction programs as well. Many medium-to-large schools and campuses have instructional development units that librarians can use to improve their teaching techniques or to develop new ones. Research and evaluation units can help to develop measurement tools, survey tools, or over-all evaluation plans. If audiovisual and graphic arts personnel are not on the library staff, outside expertise will have to be sought.

One of the fringe benefits of dealing with outsiders is that as they become aware of the ways in which the library benefits students they develop a vested interest in the success of the instruction program and become politically supportive. The extent of their involvement, of course, depends on the length of the contact and the nature of the project. It is clear, for example, that anyone who worked with the library in developing a self-paced workbook in humanities research techniques and resources is bound to learn a great deal about what the library offers. An ideal team is often a librarian, a classroom instructor, and an instructional designer.

Also an increasing number of commercial library-instruction packages are available. Librarians who rejected some early, poor-quality materials may be reluctant to consider others. Obviously, it is desirable to review the material before purchase, but it would be a serious mistake not to consider carefully the staff savings that may be provided in purchasing some instructional materials, even if inspection is impossible. Textbooks and audiovisual materials can often be adapted successfully. It is likely that the number of commercially available materials will continue to increase. One would hope that some of these will be addressed to the needs of the many small school and academic libraries that have only one or a few professionals on their staffs.

Although it is clear that librarians will always be directly involved in instruction activities, it seems likely that, as programs grow, their efforts will be limited to developing instructional materials and then teaching others to implement them. As program objectives are met and more complex goals are set, staff requirements are bound to change and new combinations will be needed.

The Head of Library Instruction

A major staffing concern in user-education programs is whether or not to designate a single person as *the* library instruction librarian. Responsibility can be given to an existing administrator (for example, the head of reader services), a new administrative post can be created, or one of the librarians can be chosen to serve a set term as coordinator. All of these models exist, and no one method has proved to be superior. Although in smaller institutions it may seem sensible to give the head of reader services responsibility for the program, unless he or she is particularly interested in library instruction or has a special aptitude for that kind of activity, it may well demand more effort than may be willingly forthcoming. What is more, putting the head of reader services in charge of the program may foreclose the possibility of involving technical services people.

To put any *one* person in charge may tend to negate the concept that the library instruction program is an integral part of the library's public services. Moreover, most people currently hired for such positions tend to be beginning-level librarians without the administrative (much less political) expertise needed to influence librarians and classroom faculty. However, given a person with the right personality traits and a library staff that is clearly committed to the program and involved with its planning, such an arrangement is quite workable. In such cases the instructional librarian usually reports to the head of reader services. Clear lines of communication are important to ensure that everyone involved in the program knows who is responsible for what, what decisions are made at what level, what to do if a conflict arises between instructional demands and other reader services (e.g., hours at the reference desk), and how instruction activities relate to other responsibilities in matters such as evaluation, promotion, and tenure. Similar guidelines will need to be established with the head of technical services if personnel from that area are to be involved in the program.

Problems will also arise where there is a coordinator for library instruction. Clear guidelines are needed to explain how and where the groups to be coordinated should be located. Is the coordinator equal in status to the head of reader services, does he or she report to that person, or is some other arrangement advisable? What is the coordinator's relationship to staff development activities or to the personnel officer? How much actual authority does he or she have over those being coordinated; how much impact on personnel evaluations? How is the division of responsibilities to be defined?

Ultimately a growing program needs a single person with a defined role, to provide leadership for the program and to handle the day-by-day issues that arise in a dynamic situation. He or she should take responsibility for ensuring that:

> Planned activities take place as needed
> Relationships with other units in the library are positive in nature
> Positive relationships are developed and maintained with support units, e.g., with the instructional development center
> Satisfactory progress is being made on all program objectives
> The quality of instruction meets acceptable standards
> Agreed-upon evaluation procedures are implemented
> Staff development activities necessary for the positive growth of the program are provided
> Records of instruction activities are maintained
> No instruction activity is missed due to scheduling conflicts or illness

Some of these responsibilities may be shared with members of a committee, but a single person should be held accountable and should be given the authority necessary for its implementation. Obviously, such responsibilities require previous experience as a librarian as well as experience in library instruction.

The decision to have a library instruction librarian or a library instruction coordinator will depend on the program's stage of development. When the program is small, "library instruction librarian" is a proper designation. A person with this title may, of course, also be asked to work with a committee in planning expansion and developing program goals and objectives.

Once the program has clearly defined goals and is large enough to require logistical planning and scheduling, the title "coordinator for library instruction" would seem appropriate. This title also suggests the library liaison roles that will develop along with an instruction program. Where there are liaison librarians, who assume responsibilities within specified academic areas for faculty contact, collection development, and library instruction, it makes organizational sense to use the title "coordinator."

Standing Committee on Library Instruction

No matter what sort of officer is directly responsible for the instruction program, it is advisable to have a standing committee on library instruction. The committee should be limited to a workable size, and each member should assume responsibility for informing specified groups of library employees about plans, progress, etc. One of the main purposes of the committee, in fact, should be the integration of the library instruction program into the everyday consciousness of the entire library staff. The committee should also serve as a focal point for real or perceived problems or issues. Depending upon the duties assigned to the person directly in charge, the committee may itself have some responsibilities for planning, evaluating, and implementing the program.

Interlibrary Cooperation

In seeking ways to make limited staffing go farther, the area of interlibrary cooperation holds much promise for user-education programs. Mention has already been made of the availability of instruction materials through library instruction clearinghouses. Cooperation between school and public libraries in programs for children has long been commonplace.

National cooperative efforts have taken place in both the United States and Britain. The efforts of the American Library Association Library Instruction Round Table to provide a societal and educational framework for user-education programs and to identify and analyze sequential programs represent necessary efforts that could not be accomplished on a local basis, much less by an individual library. After considerable study, the

British Library established the position of coordinator of library instruction activities.[4] Both of these national undertakings are concerned with user-education programs in all types of libraries.

Cooperation among libraries within a region or a state can help in other ways. Consideration should be given to developing learning matrices in conjunction with other institutions. After general agreement among a group of academic libraries about the list of groups to be served, one institution might take responsibility for science programs, another for social science programs, etc. In this case the majors offered by each institution should be kept in mind, as it is easier to eliminate items in areas not offered than to start from scratch. Another approach would be to have committees of representatives from several different institutions work on a particular set of matrices.

Cooperation can also help meet needs for instructional materials and staff development. In England academic libraries joined together to produce a series of tape-slide instructional packages.[5] A group of small academic libraries in central Illinois found it advantageous to pool their staff development needs and resources. Each year one of four joint workshops dealt with library instruction, including the use of audiovisuals and ways of developing faculty-librarian relationships. Certainly it is to be hoped that such cooperative efforts are only preludes to more extensive local cooperation in support of programs of library instruction.

There are no hard-and-fast rules for the best organizational arrangement for a library instruction program or for the establishment of staffing patterns. Some sort of liaison within school and academic settings is, however, generally advisable. More often than not, a successful user-education program will use a variety of people in changing relationships dictated by the particular developmental phase of the program and the particular learning need being addressed. Imagination should be employed and flexibility maintained, for as the program develops both organizational and staffing changes may be desirable. Three guidelines, however, should remain constant for all library instruction: the library instruction program must be an integral part of the library's services; widespread involvement in planning for the program is highly desirable; and cooperation with other libraries in both planning and implementation stages can help extend limited resources.

It should also be noted that there is a great deal of similarity in the planning and implementation processes for library instruction and staff development programs. Indeed, the library's needs for staff development should be met with the same efforts for good instructional planning that are called for in the user-education program. In small or medium-sized libraries, this similarity is a reason to combine into one job description responsibility for library instruction and staff development.

12. Public Relations

Public relations—educating potential users to available resources and services—is an integral part of the library instruction program. It has, in fact, a dual aspect: not only does a successful program of library instruction require supportive public relations efforts, but some components of the program are directed toward making users aware of the manifold ways in which the library serves the community.

By their very nature library user-education programs are the antithesis of passive librarianship. At the heart of the concept is the belief that libraries and library resources are to be exploited effectively and that those who have some fundamental knowledge about them and understand how they are organized are more likely to benefit from their services. There is, in fact, much evidence to indicate "that perceived ease of use may be the major criterion considered in selecting an information source and the overriding factor influencing whether or not a particular information service is used."[1] One academic librarian was fond of saying that so far as she was concerned a library instruction program was successful if people learned from it that they had a right to a good level of public library service and could bang their fists and demand service if not enough was forthcoming.

The infrequent use of libraries has significant implications about the quality of people's education. The fact that a great number, if not the majority, of undergraduate students can successfully complete their academic pursuits with a very limited use of books,[2] much less libraries, raises serious educational questions and bodes little good for their future reading and learning habits. Accessibility of books is known to promote reading,[3] and experiments such as Daniel Fader's work in supplying institutionalized youngsters with paperback books have had remarkable success.[4] The value of access to books is not a newly discovered truth, but educators

119

and librarians often need to be reminded of its importance. As far back as 1936, Douglas Waples admonished, "The educational importance of certain libraries is so clearly due to the intelligent promotion of student reading that the extent of such promotion should become a measure of library excellence."[5] An important indirect benefit of public relations and library instruction efforts aimed at attracting nonusers into the library, then, is the promotion of lifelong reading habits, which leads, in turn, to increased library use (and, it is hoped, to improved library support in the future).

Positive, affective responses are important in turning nonusers into users. It is not sufficient to have people know what, in a general sense, libraries have to offer in the way of resources and services. They must feel welcome in the library; they must believe that the library is a manageable and comfortable place, that librarians are friendly and have a great deal of useful knowledge to share, and that the library can be a source of information, exploration, and enjoyment. These are the concepts the instruction program should seek to project. It should create positive learning experiences for people who use the library and to entice nonusers to give it a try.

Most material dealing with public relations and publicity for libraries pertains to the public library. The *Wilson Library Bulletin*, for example, devotes one issue each year to this topic. Traditional publicity efforts will continue to be the mainstay of the public library's effort to bring its message to the total community that is it's constituency.

School and academic libraries, however, require different kinds of public relations approaches. One prime target for publicity regarding the instruction program is new faculty members. It is usually possible to arrange to receive notification of new faculty appointments. A letter can be sent from the head of the library welcoming new faculty in advance of their arrival, highlighting one or two library services and informing them of the name of the librarian who will be their chief contact person and who will be getting in touch with them to offer assistance. If there is to be a new-faculty orientation program, a segment might be reserved for the library—preferably to be held there—to cover the most pressing concerns (e.g., how to put books on reserve, how to schedule AV equipment and order films). Backup materials can be distributed. If this occasion can include an informal interaction with librarians—possibly over refreshments—so much the better. The next step, of course, is for librarians to call upon individual faculty members.

A liaison, a librarian with a particular responsibility for a specified group of faculty, allows for ongoing opportunities for public relations. As problems or issues arise and as curricula change, the ability of the library to respond quickly to needs for collection development and changing emphases in the instruction program will clearly testify to its readiness to support faculty and department activities. Moreover, librarians can use attendance at the departmental meetings as well as memos or specially prepared brief newsletters to keep faculty informed of new resources and available services, changing library hours, or other concerns that may affect them and their students, as well as to elicit feedback.

Nor should more informal aspects of public relations be overlooked. Knowing faculty, administrators, board members, etc., on a social level can allow for the sharing of key information and can establish a base that may serve as valuable leverage at some later time. More important, personal contact is bound to enhance understanding and appreciation of the librarian's role and the challenges he or she faces in fulfilling it. Such informal relationships, however, should complement formal contacts but never be considered a substitute for them.

Library advisory committees made up of faculty and students and Friends groups can provide ongoing opportunities for positive public relations. However, they will require large amounts of staff time, usually at senior levels, and the advisability of promoting such groups if they do not already exist should be weighed carefully against the anticipated benefits.

Like all other aspects of the instruction program, the public relations efforts of the library should be carefully thought out, and objectives established and evaluated. One of the first planning concerns is to identify the image that the library wishes to project. For example, because part of the image of any library should be that of competence and professionalism, all publications and correspondence should be consistent in quality and style, and should have compatible formats, typefaces, graphics, as well as perhaps a logo. Once an image has been agreed upon, all efforts to publicize particular services of the library should be geared to project it. The library at San Jose State University, for example, has adopted an attractive logo for its user-education program, featuring an arched dolphin and the acronym LEAP (Library Education and Assistance Program). This logo identifies the program in a positive, easy-to-remember fashion. To leap is to move up and forward; the action is associated with the dolphin, an animal that elicits happy responses from people. Thus, the user-education program is a way for students to move forward in their academic pursuits in a pleasurable manner.

The objectives set for the publicity program should be in keeping with library-wide objectives for the year in general. If the library is going through a reassessment and planning process, it may be decided that whatever publicity is initiated should be limited to encouraging use of the library. Certainly if new services are going to be offered or if there are plans to expand library instruction, a carefully thought-out public relations effort should be developed and implemented.

Where established avenues for publicity exist, it is useful to determine how they can be utilized to meet public relations objectives. Possibilities will generally include the institution's academic catalogs, any newsletter put out by related groups, and student or community newspapers or broadcasting stations, as well as a variety of activities generated by the public relations office.

Learning experiences must be carefully structured if users are not to be overwhelmed. On the other hand, the more that can be done in the way of publicizing the successes of user-education programs, the better. Clear statistical proofs of student retention or academic success related to library instruction are especially helpful. A student letter or feature article for the student newspaper regarding some aspect of the program that students have found beneficial is another possible vehicle. A faculty member might share his or her ideas about motivating students to use the library at a brown-bag lunch. A mother might tell a social or church group what the public library has meant to her children's schoolwork. Results can also be presented more formally in annual reports or in special reports to academic administrators, faculty, and boards.

Since people cannot learn everything they need to know about the library in one instructional experience, the public relations program must be concerned that the library is an attractive or at least comfortable place, to which people will want to return. Poor lighting, drab colors, overcrowded furniture, or overwhelming spaces are hardly inviting. If it is impossible to create an attractive atmosphere throughout the library, try for attractive lounge areas next to the stacks. Is there a place nearby where people can go to smoke and eat? Are there group study areas? Although a library staff can generally do little to improve building structures, the library instruction effort should lead to good sign systems, color coding, and the establishment, if need be, of service points, where directions can be given.[6]

Enticements that have traditionally been characteristic activities of public libraries may well be used to attract people into the academic library. Are new or popular reading books strategically located so as to attract browsers? Could a paperback take-one-leave-one rack, if publicized, bring more people into the library? What about art exhibits, film previewings, brown-bag luncheon programs featuring local speakers for informal talks, or musical performances at noon or dinner hours in a lounge area? All of these possibilities can enhance the library's image as a dynamic, interesting place to go. Once there, people may discover and use other services and resources. This ploy is what department stores have been using for years; they offer special sales to attract customers, knowing that once there, most customers will purchase other goods.

At times the boundary lines between public relations and library instruction will seem fuzzy and roles will overlap, particularly in promoting the use of libraries by nonusers. Both the public relations and instruction activities of a library require ongoing planning and evaluation if they are to prosper, and both need to be clearly related to over-all goals. Certainly library user-education programs need to be promoted by a combination of formal and informal methods if they are to grow and expand.

13. The Instructional Mission in the Eighties

Concern for the instructional mission of libraries is both old and new. The original proponents of an instructional mission came from the field of higher education, but the recognition of the importance of libraries to the whole educational enterprise continues today. The pioneers were a handful of visionary librarians, notably, Otis Robinson, Harvie Branscomb, Lamar Johnson, and Patricia Knapp. Their leadership goes back as far as the 1870s when Robinson was admonishing the profession: "All that is taught in college amounts to very little; but if we can send students out self-reliant in their investigations, we have accomplished very much."[1] Despite such early direction and inspiration, it has taken the down-to-earth, concrete, library user-education programs of the 1970s planned and implemented by librarians across the United States and in Britain, to win a foothold for library instruction in education. It is these programs that will serve as the foundation for the expansion of the educational function of libraries during the eighties.

General Trends

To summarize the current situation and anticipate upcoming efforts will, therefore, to some degree define the mission for the eighties. To begin with, it is safe to say that library instruction is here to stay. Indeed, it has become so highly institutionalized within the library profession and within a growing number of disciplines that it would be quite difficult to get rid of it even if that were a desirable thing to do.[2] The formalized support base, moreover, derives from the complex information-handling capabilities so integral to twentieth-century living. Their impact was succinctly summed up in a British workshop on "The Education of Users of Scientific and Technical Information" in 1973:

> [Information handling] is integral to education and to communication, linked to the reception of information at one end and at the other to the communication of information to others, a key factor in the development of alert and critical minds.[3]

The centrality of information-handling makes library instruction equally at home with back-to-basics movements in education—wherein the right of access to and ability to use resources becomes the fourth R—and with movements toward liberalizing requirements—wherein individualized learning efforts are enriched by access to the literature of all ages and disciplines. To conclude that trends and needs in education demand library user-education programs is not merely politicking; it is also reality.

Library user-education programs will face the same problems of tightening budgets and increasing demands for accountability that will continue to face all other aspects of education. It is interesting to note that in the March 1980 *Journal of Academic Librarianship* column of opinion on the future patterns of library user-education programs, four of the five responses directly commented on budget and accountability concerns. Major sources of soft money for support of individual instruction programs are largely gone,[4] and the reallocating of funds for user-education programs from other areas in the library and on the campus will continue to be very difficult.

However, several trends will help to mitigate the scarcity of resources. First, an increase in good-quality, commercially produced library instruction materials will eliminate the need for expensive duplication of effort. Second, libraries will increasingly find ways of cooperating in the area of library instruction. Just as it is now unthinkable for a library to contemplate developing all of its automated systems in-house, so will cooperation in instruction become an increasingly attractive and necessary way of moving such efforts forward. Third, libraries will become more realistic about aspirations for their user-education programs. The programs cannot be all things to all people, and libraries will become increasingly better at targeting their efforts in order to produce the best and most comprehensive results.

Factors other than funds will play an even greater role in the success of library user-education programs. There will, in fact, be a growing variance in the quality of programs, the internal commitment to library instruction, the amount of time put into planning and evaluation, and the degree to which the imagination of library personnel can be brought to bear. Where solid commitment exists, organizational patterns will have to reflect the changing needs of those involved in the program, and more than likely new promotional lines will have to be developed alongside the traditional supervisory/management ones. This trend should not be particularly difficult in academic libraries, since with expanded instructional roles librarians will often be subject to faculty criteria for promotion and tenure. The role of technical services librarians requires attention, too. While the involvement of technical services people in the program may represent a positive response to staff savings created by automated systems, a problematic blurring of lines of authority between public and technical services may occur. The commitment of library staff and the imaginative and creative use of existing resources will make or break most library user-education programs. As success builds on success in some programs, a familiar biblical adage will take on practical overtones: "For to every one who has will more be given, and he will have abundance; but from him who has not, even what he has will be taken away (Matthew 25:29)."

Major Developments to Come

Beyond these general trends, which are already well under way, the coming decade will evidence two major developments in library instruction. Cooperative efforts at national, regional, and state levels should lead to the development of a series of models for user-education programs. The models will range from the theoretical ones being developed by the ALA Library Instruction Round Table, to standardized curricula and tests for library instruction in public school systems, and to well-developed, innovative practicing models. While the theoretical models are important for discussion with other professions and potential clients, and while standardized programs at the public school level will to some degree also facilitate the development of related learning ladders at the college level, it is the practicing models that will be the most powerful agents for change.

The value of practicing or demonstration models was underscored at the British workshop noted earlier in this chapter. The conference recommended that, since change normally occurs because a few pioneers lead the way, encouraging others by their success, an effort should be made to identify institutions where people and the environment are favorable to innovation in library instruction.[5] A major commitment of funds to these institutions from a foundation or a group of foundations in a program coordinated under the leadership of the American Library Association or its divisions could then mean major breakthroughs in the conceptualization, implementation, and evaluation of user-education programs by providing a series of demonstration models in a variety of settings. Without such outside funding the models will take much longer to develop and will, perhaps, be more limited in their effects. However, model programs of various sizes and complexities will emerge as libraries develop growing commitments to their educational functions.

There is one precedent for the establishment of such models. In 1962, $1,130,000 was allocated by the Knapp Foundation to create living examples of the recommendations in the 1960 *Standards for School Library Programs*, to see what types of school library services would, in fact, emerge if money were not a deterrent. The final results of this project were published by the American Library Association in the book entitled *Realization: The Final Report of the Knapp School Library Project*.[6] The eight school library programs described in this book probably did more than any single activity of that decade to demonstrate to librarians, teachers, administrators, and parents what dynamic school library programs could mean to quality education. Similarly, the decade of the eighties is the time for models offering a variety of library user-education programs to stimulate and challenge the profession and those it seeks to serve.

On the academic level, for example, a handful of libraries from representative institutions (i.e., the undergraduate library at a large university, a community college library, a library at a small private institution, the library at an inner-city nonresidential institution, and one or two others) could be chosen according to several criteria: (1) library and institutional commitments to an expanded educational role for the library; (2) an existing planned user-education program; and (3) a location suitable for providing easy access for demonstration. The involvement of a teacher-education institution—coupled with a program of visitation, evaluation, and reporting like that articulated in the Knapp School Library Project—could well produce a serious and lasting impact for a relatively reasonable investment. Such models could provide some concrete answers to long-standing questions regarding how and to what degree information-handling skills can promote student retention and academic success.

Assuming the continued development of the library instruction movement, the second major trend in the coming decade—albeit a very slow one—will be a change in emphasis from academic libraries to school and, in some circumstances, public libraries. The ability to handle information effectively is simply too important to be postponed until college years. Moreover, a large percentage of the population either does not go to college or delays further education for a number of years. This change in focus has already begun in England. The British Library, which now has an officer to coordinate user education, decided after considerable study that in the future special funding and research activities will focus on library user education within the public school system.[7] The public school situation in the United States is, of course, much more complex. For all practical purposes, it is not coordinated; yet, where adequate school systems do exist, every attempt must be made to stimulate positive library-use patterns and thereby to promote reading. Where school libraries are lacking or where school systems fail, the public library must bridge the gap. Ultimately, all library instruction should result in lifelong public library use. This change in emphasis will not mean less library instruction activity in academic libraries, but rather it will reflect a growing acceptance among the general public and among educators of the importance of effective information handling in the education of young people. It will also mean that the learning objectives for college-level instruction will have to be modified to build on efforts at the secondary level.

Four Major Tasks

Four major tasks face libraries attempting to develop quality user-education programs in the 1980s. First, libraries must better define for themselves the role their instruction programs are to play. On the one hand, the public library role is likely to become broader, to encompass everything from the traditional children's story hour (as a means of promoting reading), to expanding literacy courses, reader and learner advisory services, and more extensive joint instruction programs with local school systems and academic institutions. Roles will have to be defined not by function but by the groups of people to be served. The school and academic libraries that are developing quality instruction programs will narrow the focus of their instruction activities to programs that directly support the goals of their parent institutions and that libraries are uniquely qualified to address. Librarians in these institutions are, in fact, far better able to support the over-all educational goals of their parent institutions than are classroom instructors. In particular, librarians should be concerned with the promotion of reading and the preparation of people for lifelong learning through developing the habit of using libraries. The emphasis must increasingly be on attitudinal development rather than on subject or skill mastery.

The second major task will be to interpret the instructional role to the funding sources, legislatures, and the communities. Well-developed public relations programs will be essential for all types of libraries. School and academic libraries must project a new image and gain acceptance of a model for quality education that, though not new, is not widely accepted. Figure 16 depicts a model based on a three-person team comprised of the classroom instructor, the librarian, and the media expert. Such teamwork can be extremely supportive of quality instruction: the instructor determines desired learning outcomes, the librarian identifies available resources and the means by which they can be exploited, and the media person designs and produces needed learning packages and instructional aids. This coordinated approach not only provides individualized learning experiences to facilitate students' acquisition of lifelong learning skills, but should also create a dynamic learning situation in which faculty development for all three professional groups takes place on an ongoing basis.

The service patterns of special libraries should become more familiar at universities as pressures for accountability continue, and the inclusion of librarians on research teams should become as expected as the presence of librarians in the classroom.

The third and fourth major tasks facing libraries will be to evaluate their success in fulfilling their roles and to gain widespread acceptance of that role. These two points have already been discussed, but in light of the fact that the Hungarian Minister of Education mandated eight to ten hours in instruction in literature searching at the academic level,[8] the aim of gaining widespread endorsement for including the acquisition of information-handling/research capabilities in formal education is not unrealistic for democratic countries that pride themselves on an informed citizenry. Support from educational and other professional groups should be sought. It cannot be underscored too strongly that the necessary preliminary step to such acceptance is the evaluation of the educational effectiveness of the library, rather than the size of its collection or its administrative efficiency.

The Mission

Back in the 1930s one institution, Stephens College, was practicing what most of us are still just dreaming and preaching about today. The librarian of the college wrote, "The activities of librarians become meaningless unless they actually effect changes in teaching and learning."[9] The instructional mission of libraries in the eighties is to effect changes *for the better* in the teaching and learning patterns throughout the country.

The rationale necessitating just such a challenge for librarians was given in Chapter 1. It appears more than likely that the major problems facing education today cannot be fully met unless librarians become more active

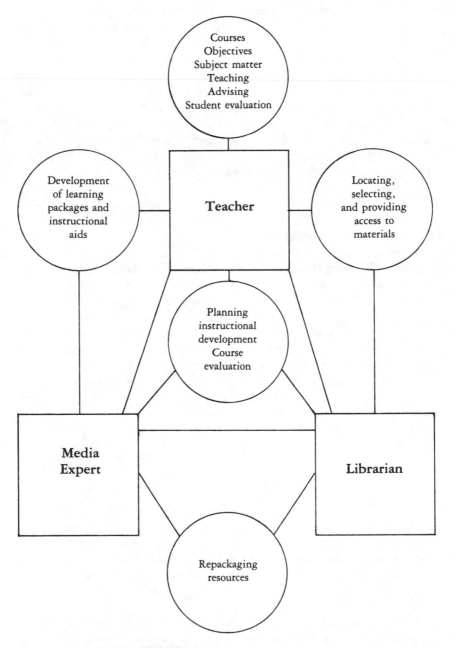

Figure 16.   Model of quality education

members of the educational team. Individualizing the learning process and preparing people for lifelong learning are necessary, but little progress will be made without the active involvement of librarians in both the planning and implementation stages of instruction at all levels of education.

In the months and years ahead, some libraries will make plans to pursue these educational goals systematically. For example, the Auraria Library, which serves three academic institutions in downtown Denver, adopted the following goals early in 1980:

> To promote increased use of library resources as a means of enhancing the learning/teaching process.
>
> 1) To relate library services to changes in the student body and in curricular offerings.
> 2) To increase the faculty's knowledge and use of the library's human, material, and other resources.
> 3) To involve library and teaching faculty in efforts to explore more effective ways of achieving instructional objectives.
> 4) To assist students in becoming more effective users of information.

The statement is, of course, an ambitious one. Its enormity fully registered in April 1980 when, as the library's new director, I prepared to speak about the instructional mission of academic libraries to a statewide conference in Colorado. The program took place the week following the state of Colorado's budgeting process in which serious staffing cuts had occurred at both small and large academic libraries. Having heard story after story about the effects the cuts would cause, it almost seemed inhuman to suggest *any* service mission, much less one designed to affect teaching and learning patterns.

The term "mission," which brought to mind images of sacrifice and attempts to do the impossible, became the pivotal concept. It is just these connotations, in fact, that are most applicable to the challenge of library instruction. Is there something so important about the educational function of libraries that, despite severe limitations on staffs and resources, it must be developed? The answer is yes. Libraries have a unique role to play in addressing the needs of education today, and unless librarians become more active members of the educational team, significant issues such as individualizing learning will remain unachieved goals.

Not every library or every librarian is in the position to develop a full program of library user education. But what is important, in fulfilling a mission, is that everyone does what one can and a little more. The failure of the Montieth Experiment, which in many ways is responsible for much that is good in current library instruction, is worth noting. The faculty recruited for the experiment ultimately found it impossible to change its teaching styles. Yet the failure has been one of the most positive occurrences in library instruction. Moreover, Patricia Knapp, who directed that project, like many individuals who have been committed to an expanded educational role for libraries, had a profound effect on the individuals with whom she came in contact. For example, the president of Earlham College and the founding president of Sangamon State University, both of whom were active supporters of teaching libraries, were both influenced by her. Perhaps all that an individual librarian can hope to do in one year is to enlarge one teacher's vision of what a library is and what it can offer by way of support for education, yet the full value of the contact never can be fully known. Whether it is influencing one person or developing a full-scale plan for a library user-education program, each library must be part of the mission of the eighties and commit itself to some instructional accomplishment.

Crucial to the accomplishment of the library's instructional mission are the three C's: conviction, commitment, and cooperation. *Conviction* that libraries have a unique and significant contribution to make in the provision of quality education; *commitment* to plan and evaluate, to get the job done, to confront the necessary and painful reallocation of resources; *cooperation within* the library to affirm that instruction must be an integral part of library services, and *cooperation among* professionals from different libraries so that each may benefit from the other's mistakes and accomplishments so that resources may be effectively utilized in the decades ahead. A sound instruction program will improve both teaching and learning.

Appendix

Guidelines for Bibliographic Instruction in Academic Libraries

The college and university library performs a unique and indispensable function in the educational process. It bears the central responsibility for developing the college and university library collections; for extending bibliographic control over these collections; for instructing students formally and informally; and for advising faculty and scholars in the use of these collections.

In order to assist college and university libraries in the planning and evaluation of effective programs to instruct members of the academic community in the identification and use of information resources, the following guidelines for bibliographic instruction in academic libraries are suggested:

The library should:

(1)   assess the needs of its academic community for orientation to the library's facilities and services, and for instruction in the use of the library's collections and bibliographic structure;

(2)   prepare a written profile of the community's information needs;

(3)   develop a written statement of objectives of bibliographic instruction which:

    (a)   includes immediate and long-range goals with a projected timetable for implementation;

    (b)   is directed to specific identified needs within the academic community, and permits various methods of instruction for

Reprinted from the April 1977 issue of *College & Research Libraries News*, a publication of the Association of College and Research Libraries.

all segments of the academic community who have a need to use library resources and services;

(c) outlines methods by which progress toward the attainment of instructional objectives can be measured. Methodology must provide for measures of learning.

(4) provide continuing financial support for bibliographic instruction,

(a) clearly identifiable within the library's budget program and statements;

(b) sufficient to provide the professional and supportive staff, equipment, materials, and facilities necessary to attain the delineated objectives.

(5) employ librarians and other qualified staff to plan, implement, and evaluate the program,

(a) inclusive of persons with training in: various academic disciplines, the identification and use of library resources, teaching skills, preparation and use of audiovisual and other instructional materials, preparation and use of evaluative instruments, clerical skill;

(b) in sufficient numbers necessary to attain the delineated objectives;

(c) clearly identifiable and of a status appropriate to persons responsible for planning, implementing, and evaluating the other major functions of the library;

(6) provide facilities, equipment, and materials

(a) to accommodate the preparation of instructional materials and the presentation of various modes of instruction (individual, small or large group, lecture, discussion, media, etc.);

(b) of sufficient size, number, and scope to accommodate the attainment of the delineated objectives;

(7) involve the academic community in the formulation of objectives and the evaluation of their attainment;

(8) evaluate regularly the effectiveness of the instructional program, and demonstrate substantial attainment of written objectives.

Notes

Introduction

1. Edward G. Holley, "Academic Libraries in 1976," in *Libraries for Teaching: Libraries for Research*, ed. Richard D. Johnson (Chicago: ALA, 1977), p. 1.

2. William M. Randall, *The College Library: A Descriptive Study of the Libraries in Four Year Liberal Arts Colleges in the United States* (Chicago: ALA and the University of Chicago Press, 1932), p. 142.

3. Carnegie Commission on Higher Education, *Reform on Campus: Changing Students, Changing Academic Programs* (New York: The Commission, 1972), p. 50.

4. Position statements issued at the second Conference on Integrating the Library into the Educational Mainstream, University of Wisconsin at Parkside, June 1978 (unpublished).

5. K. Patricia Cross, "Libraries in the Learning Society," speech made to the Library Instruction Round Table meeting at the ALA Annual Conference, Dallas, Texas, June 26, 1979.

6. Jean Brooks, "User Education in Public Libraries," speech given in a panel discussion on User Education Activities in Texas, Texas Library Association Conference, Houston, April 8, 1976 (unpublished proceedings), p. 23.

Chapter 1

1. Patricia Senn Breivik, "Library Instruction and Instructional Development," in *Library Instruction and Faculty Development: Growth Opportunities in the Academic Community*, ed. Nyal Z. Williams and Jack T. Tsukamoto (Ann Arbor, Mich.: Pierian Press, 1980), pp. 29–36.

2. Howard R. Bowen, "The Residue of Academic Learning," 3rd in a series of excerpts from *Investment in Learning: The Individual and Social Value of*

American Education (San Francisco: Jossey-Bass, 1977), *The Chronicle of Higher Education* 15 (November 14, 1977):13.

3. Frank Spikes, "The UNESCO Recommendations on Adult Education: Implications for Practice in the U.S.," *Lifelong Learning: The Adult Years* 2 (April 1979):5.

4. Walter F. Mondale, "The Next Step: Lifelong Learning," *Change* 8 (October 1976):42–45.

5. Comments made by Franklin Wallin, president, Earlham College, at the second Conference on Integrating the Library into the Educational Mainstream, University of Wisconsin at Parkside, June 1978 (unpublished).

6. Comments made by Daniel Johnson at the Conference on Integrating the Library into the Educational Mainstream, Sangamon State (Ill.) University, June 1977 (unpublished).

Chapter 2

1. Larry Hardesty, "Instructional Development in Library Use Education," in *Improving Library Instruction: How to Teach and How to Evaluate*, ed. Carolyn A. Kirkendall (Ann Arbor, Mich.: Pierian Press, 1979), pp. 11–35.

Chapter 3

1. Patricia Senn Breivik, ed., *Objective Setting for Illinois Libraries* (Chicago: Illinois Library Association, April 1978).

2. Robert Cronson, "Finite Revenue Pie," *IACRL Newsletter* 5 (Summer 1979):12.

3. Morris Hamburg, Leonard E. Ramist, and Michael R. W. Bommer, "Library Objectives and Performance Measures and Their Use in Decision Making," *Library Quarterly* 42 (January 1972):108.

4. Jean Brooks, "User Education in Public Libraries," speech given in a panel discussion on User Education Activities in Texas, Texas Library Association Conference, Houston, April 8, 1976 (unpublished proceedings), p. 23.

5. James F. Govan, "Community Analysis in an Academic Environment," *Library Trends* 24 (January 1976):54–56.

6. Harvie Branscomb, *Teaching with Books* (Chicago: American Association of American Colleges and ALA, 1940), p. 198.

Chapter 4

1. Jacob M. Price, ed., *Reading for Life* (Ann Arbor: University of Michigan Press, 1959), pp. 253–54.

2. Jean Brooks, "User Education in Public Libraries," speech given in a panel discussion on User Education Activities in Texas, Texas Library Association Conference, Houston, April 8, 1976.

3. Anne S. Mavor, Jose Orlando Toro, and Ernest R. DeProspo, *Final Report: The Role of the Public Libraries in Adult Independent Learning*, parts 1 and 2 (New York: College Entrance Examination Board, 1976).

4. "Literacy: Wrong Job for Libraries? *L.J. Hotlines* 8 (December 10, 1979):5.

Chapter 6

1. William Watson Parkey, *Self Concept and School Achievement* (Englewood Cliffs, N.J.: Prentice-Hall, 1970), pp. v–vi.

2. Mignon Adams, "Effects of Evaluation on Teaching Methods," in *Improving Library Instruction: How to Teach and Evaluate*, ed. Carolyn A. Kirkendall (Ann Arbor, Mich.: Pierian Press, 1979), p. 98.

3. "The Education of Users of Scientific and Technical Information," report from a workshop held at the University of Bath, September 14–16, 1973, (Bath University Library, 1973), p. 14.

4. John R. Lincoln, "Latent Image Technology for Feedback in Library Instruction," in *Improving Library Instruction: How to Teach and Evaluate*, ed. Carolyn A. Kirkendall (Ann Arbor, Mich.: Pierian Press, 1979), p. 81.

5. Jerome S. Bruner, "The Act of Discovery," *Harvard Educational Review* 31 (Winter 1961):21–32.

6. Harvie Branscomb, *Teaching with Books* (Chicago: Association of American Colleges and ALA, 1940), p. 207.

Chapter 7

1. Robert F. Mager, *Preparing Instructional Objectives*, 2nd ed. (Belmont, Calif.: Fearon Publishers, 1975).

2. Jacquelyn M. Morris and Donald F. Webster, *Developing Objectives for Library Instruction* (New York: New York Library Assn., 1976).

3. Marvin E. Wiggins, "A Scientific Model for the Development of Library Use Instruction Programs," in *A Challenge for Academic Libraries: How to Motivate Students to Use the Library*, ed. Sul H. Lee (Ann Arbor, Mich.: Pierian Press, 1973), pp. 21–46.

Chapter 8

1. R. R. Ronkin, "A Self-Guided Library Tour for the Biosciences," *College and Research Libraries* 28 (May 1967): 218.

2. Peter Hernon, "Library Lectures and Their Evaluation: A Survey," *The Journal of Academic Librarianship*, 1 (July 1975): 15–16.

3. Alice B. Griffith, "*Library Handbook Standards*," *College and Research Libraries* 39 (February 1965):475–77.

4. "Library Instruction—The Right Time and Place," *Journal of Academic Librarianship* 4 (May 1978):90–91.

5. Katherine G. Cipolla, "M.I.T.'s Point-of-Use Concept: A Five-Year Update," *Journal of Academic Librarianship* 5 (January 1980):326.

6. Judith L. Violette, "Library Instruction with Slides and Slide/Tapes," in *Improving Library Instruction*, ed. Carolyn A. Kirkendall (Ann Arbor, Mich.: Pierian Press, 1979), pp. 85–86.

7. Malcolm Fleming and W. Howard Levie, *Instructional Message Design: Principles from the Behavioral Sciences* (Englewood Cliffs, N.J.: Educational Technology, 1978), p. 107.

8. Beverly L. R. Renford, "A Self-Paced Workbook for Beginning College Students," *Journal of Academic Librarianship* 4 (September 1978):200–203.

9. Marvin E. Wiggins, "The Development of Library Use Instructional Programs," *College and Research Libraries* 33 (November 1972) 473–79.

10. See, for example, Marvin E. Wiggins, "A Scientific Model for the Development of Library Use Instructional Programs" in *A Challenge for Academic Libraries: How to Motivate Students to Use the Library*, ed. Sul H. Lee (Ann Arbor, Mich.: Pierian Press, 1973), pp. 21–46.

11. John R. Lincoln, "Latent Image Technology for Feedback in Library Instruction," in *Improving Library Instruction: How to Teach and How to Evaluate*, ed. Carolyn A. Kirkendall (Ann Arbor, Mich.: Pierian Press, 1979), pp. 77–82.

12. Wiggins, "The Development of Library Use Instructional Materials," p. 476.

13. James E. Espich and Bill Williams, *Developing Programmed Instructional Materials* (Belmont, Calif.: Fearon Publishers, 1967), p. 6.

14. Linda L. Phillips and E. Ann Raup, "Comparing Methods for Teaching Use of Periodical Indexes," *Journal of Academic Librarianship* 4 (January 1979):420–23.

15. Patricia B. Culkin, "Computer-Based Public Access Systems: A Forum for Library Instruction," *Drexel Library Quarterly* 16 (January 1980):69–82.

Chapter 9

1. Hazel Mews, *Reader Instruction in Colleges and Universities* (London: Clive Bingley, 1972), pp. 17–25.

2. Frederic R. Hartz, "Freshman Library Orientation: A Need for New Approaches," *College and Research Libraries* 26 (May 1965):227–231.

3. Hugh Pritchard, "Pre-Arrival Library Instruction for College Students," *College and Research Libraries* 26 (July 1965):321.

Chapter 10

1. Policy and Planning Committee, Bibliographic Instruction Section, Association of College and Research Libraries, ALA, "Academic Biblio-

graphic Instruction: Model Statement of Objectives," in *Bibliographic Instruction Handbook* (Chicago: The Committee, 1979), pp. 35–45.

2. Thomas Kirk, "Bibliographic Instruction—A Review of Research," in *Evaluating Library Use Instruction*, ed. Richard J. Beeler (Ann Arbor, Mich.: Pierian Press, 1975), pp. 28–29.

3. Ibid., pp. 24–27.

4. B. Lamar Johnson, *Librarian and the Teacher in General Education: A Report of Library Instructional Activities at Stephens College* (Chicago: ALA, 1948).

5. Patrick Barkey, "Patterns of Student Use of a College Library," *College and Research Libraries* 26 (March 1965):115.

6. Lloyd A. Kramer and Martha B. Kramer, "The College Library and the Drop Out," *College and Research Libraries* 31 (July 1968):310.

7. Daniel N. Fader and Elton B. McNeil, *Hooked on Books: Program and Proof* (New York: Berkeley Publishing Corp., 1968).

8. Susan Burton, "Objective Tests as an Evaluation Tool: Problems in Construction and Use," in *Library Instruction in the Seventies: State of the Art*, ed. Hannelore B. Rader (Ann Arbor, Mich.: Pierian Press, 1977), pp. 99–103.

Chapter 11

1. Patricia Senn Breivik, "A Model for Library Management," *LJ Special Report* no. 10 (Summer 1979):4–9.

2. Pauline Wilson, "Librarians as Teachers: The Study of an Organized Fiction," *Library Quarterly* 49 (April 1979):146–162.

3. Carolyn Kirkendall, ed., "Library Instruction: A Column of Opinion," *The Journal of Academic Librarianship*, 4 (May 1978):88–89.

4. The Review Committee on Education for Information Use, "Final Report" (The British Library Research Development Report No. 5325 HC, 1977), pp. 17–18.

5. Peter Fox, *Reader Instruction Methods in Academic Libraries*, 1973 (Cambridge: University Library, 1974), p. 51.

Chapter 12

1. F. W. Lancaster, *The Measurement and Evaluation of Library Services* (Washington, D.C.: Information Resources Press, 1977), pp. 312–13.

2. Peter H. Mann, *Students and Books* (London: Routledge and Kegan Paul, 1974), p. 193.

3. Robert Cooley Angell, "Reading in the Social Sciences," in *Reading for Life* ed. Jacob M. Price (Ann Arbor: University of Michigan Press, 1959), p. 121.

4. Daniel N. Fader and Elton B. McNeil. *Hooked on Books: Program and Proof* (New York: Berkeley Publishing Corp., 1968).

5. Douglas Waples, *The Library*, no. 4 in the series The Evolution of Higher Institutions (Chicago: University of Chicago Press, 1936), p. 77.

6.   See, for example, R. J. P. Carey, *Library Guiding*: *A Program for Exploiting Data* (Hamden, Conn.: Linnet Books, 1974).

Chapter 13

1.   Edward G. Holley, "Academic Libraries in 1876," in *Libraries for Teaching*: *Libraries for Research*, ed. Richard D. Johnson (Chicago: ALA, 1977), p. 1.

2.   Anne K. Beaubien, "Bibliographic Instruction within Library and Discipline Associations: A Survey of Contact Persons and Committees," report prepared by the Subcommittee on Professional Organizations, Committee on Cooperation, Bibliographic Instruction Section, Association of College and Research Libraries, June 1979 (unpublished).

3.   "The Education of Users of Scientific and Technical Information," report from a workshop held at the University of Bath, September 14–16, 1973 (Bath University Library, 1973), p. 18.

4.   Nancy E. Gwinn, "The CLR Experience: Academic Libraries and Undergraduate Education," *College and Research Libraries* 41 (January 1980): 10–11.

5.   "The Education of Users of Scientific and Technical Information," p. 20.

6.   Peggy Sullivan, ed., *Realization*: *The Final Report of the Knapp School Libraries Project* (Chicago: ALA, 1968).

7.   Terry Cannon, "Review of Past Research and Directions for Future Research," in *Library User Education*; *Are New Approaches Needed?* Proceedings of a conference, Trinity College Cambridge 1979, ed. Peter Fox. Research and Development Report no. 5503 (London: British Library, March 1980), p. 92.

8.   K. Heberger and J. Balays, "Educating the Students as Library Users in the Hungarian Technical Universities," in *Educating the Library User*: *Proceedings of the Fourth Triennial Meeting of the International Association of Technological University Libraries*, April 1–3, 1970, ed. C. M. Lincoln (Loughborough University of Technology Library: IATUL, 1970), p. c–11.

9.   B. Lamar Johnson, *The Librarian and the Teacher in General Education*: *A Report of Library Instructional Activities at Stephens College* (Chicago: ALA, 1948), p. 40.

Selected Reading List

The following books were selected either to provide an in-depth look at some aspect of the educational function of libraries or to direct readers to significant major publications that give an overview of library instruction. Materials on more specific issues may be obtained by consulting chapter notes.

Breivik, Patricia Senn. *Open Admissions and the Academic Library.* Chicago: ALA, 1977. Explores the role of information-handling skills in the academic success of educationally disadvantaged college freshmen students at Brooklyn College.

Carey, R. J. P. *Library Guiding: A Program for Exploiting Data.* Hamden, Conn.: Linnet Books, 1974. Approaches library instruction from a total systems perspective and considers the role of signage, audiovisual aids, information stations, printed guides, and the like.

Davies, Ruth Ann. *The School Library: A Force for Educational Excellence.* New York: Bowker, 1969. Explores the role of the school learning resource center as an active agent in promoting educational excellence. Provides the over-all framework in which library user-education programs should be fostered.

Fox, Peter, ed. *Library User Education; Are New Approaches Needed?* Proceedings of a conference, Trinity College, Cambridge, 1979. Research and Development Report no. 5503. London: British Library, March 1980. Papers from the first international conference on library instruction. While geared to the academic setting, the paired British and American papers provide insights into two national movements that share much in common but are far from duplicating each other.

Library Orientation Series, v. 1– , 1971– . Papers presented at the annual conferences on library orientation held at Eastern Michigan University, published by Pierian Press. Quality of the articles varies but the total series provides a fairly comprehensive view of the library instruction movement and its problems in higher education.

Lincoln, C. M., ed. *Educating the Library User: Proceedings of the Fourth Triennial Meeting of the International Association of Technological University Libraries*, April 1–3, 1970. Loughborough University of Technology Library: IATUL, 1970. Exposure to academic library instruction efforts in Europe through papers and discussion.

Monroe, Margaret E. *Library Adult Education: The Biography of an Idea.* New York: Scarecrow Press, 1963. In-depth study of the evolution of library-based adult education. Although not concerned with library instruction per se, the book provides a framework within which well-developed user-education programs should evolve in the public library setting.

Price, Jacob M., ed. *Reading for Life: Developing the College Students' Lifetime Reading Interest.* Ann Arbor: University of Michigan Press, 1959. Exploration of why college students do or do not read while in school and afterwards. Contributors include teachers, librarians, administrators, and businessmen.

Index

143